I WANT TO TALK TO YOU

I Want to Talk to You

And Other Conversations

DIANA EVANS

Chatto & Windus

LONDON

1 3 5 7 9 10 8 6 4 2

Chatto & Windus, an imprint of Vintage, is part of the
Penguin Random House group of companies

Vintage, Penguin Random House UK,
One Embassy Gardens, 8 Viaduct Gardens, London sw11 7bw

Penguin
Random House
UK

First published by Chatto & Windus in 2025

penguin.co.uk/vintage
global.penguinrandomhouse.co.uk

Typeset in 12/14.75pt Bembo Book MT Pro by Jouve (UK), Milton Keynes
Printed and bound in Great Britain by Clays Ltd, Elcograf S.p.A.

The authorised representative in the EEA is Penguin Random House Ireland,
Morrison Chambers, 32 Nassau Street, Dublin D02 yh68

A CIP catalogue record for this book is available from the British Library

HB ISBN 9781784744243
TPB ISBN 9781784744250

Penguin Random House is committed to a sustainable future
for our business, our readers and our planet. This book is made
from Forest Stewardship Council® certified paper.

Contents

Introduction: I Want to Talk to You

At a guest lecture in London, a student asked me how I found my voice. She was referring to my fiction voice, which I remember finding specifically in October 2002 in a residential area of Norwich, on the floor of an upstairs room in a student house. I had been walking up and down all day, pacing. There were bits of paper strewn across the carpet, notes from a novel-in-progress that was undergoing a major reconstruction. The voice was somewhere in there, in the bits of paper, having been stuck until then in the wrong shape. All I had to do was pick it up and take it over to my desk in the corner, where through the making of clean, successive sentences it would be rebirthed. It was a long and difficult labour, but eventually it arrived, meaning that the sentences had the right feeling and sounded the same as what was in my head.

There is another voice, the journalism voice, found sometime earlier in North Kensington, near the canal, also upstairs. This one was easier to locate because the subject, or subjects, already had a shape and texture of their own and could be seen. I could put on a record and listen to some music, read a press release, do some research or have a conversation with someone. I could see what they were wearing, their gestures as we were talking, describe the exact backdrop and life story, so the sentences knew at the start which way to go, how long it would take to get there in terms of word count, the general tone and path of detachment to tread, even if the full details of the journey were unknown. This was part of the joy of it: there was room to play and discover but the parameters were pre-marked.

The journalism voice is direct, conspicuous and definite. The fiction voice is nebulous, shadowy, prefers to disappear in order to speak.

In the early days of my writing life, these two voices seemed to belong to different parts of the day, so I would write journalism in the bright alert of morning and fiction in the shady alcoves of the afternoon, when the day was diffuse and drifting towards twilight. They depended on and complemented one another, though were also in conflict. My *true* work, I felt, was fiction, and I should give it all my attention because it is a selfish voice, greedy and all-consuming as well as jealous, forever making threats to leave if I turn away from it for too long. But what the other voice was always trying to get across was that the making of fiction needs ventilation – you can't live there all the time, it's unstable, confusing, suffocating, and can drive you crazy. I think the journalism is maybe a little younger than the fiction by nature, although they both like to have fun, in different ways. They're still arguing. They still would rather I choose between them. The fiction knows it has my heart and punishes me accordingly.

Between 2002 and 2022 I wrote four novels with mostly rising levels of difficulty. Each was written in a kind of picturesque time warp, full of great faith and perseverance, held in the enclosure of the original idea while the world went on outside. I could swim as deep as I wanted in the poetics of language. I could stretch sentences into whole paragraphs and inhabit multiple souls. The difficulty, generally, was in dealing with the scaffolding of narrative structure – there was always a pattern to serve, a bigger cohesion to refer to, everything had to make sense in relation to character and plot, all of which could feel like a hindrance to expression, even an obstruction to truth. And this goes on for a very, very long time. I would yearn for the freedom of the direct address, to be able to express an idea, image, moment or opinion briefly and succinctly without it needing to belong to a larger narrative whole. The almost monastic mode of existence required to produce the type of long-form fiction I was interested in writing ultimately proved to be unsustainable without sporadic forays into journalism, that beautiful sphere of brevity and solidity, where a piece could be complete in a week, where I knew exactly what was going to happen to it and I could say exactly what I wanted to say. Often when I was approached by an editor to write something – an interview with a musician, a review of an exhibition or a cover story – the fiction voice would cry, *Don't do it!* Then it would complain of neglect and potential ruin all the way through, causing some occupational discomfort. But I would return when it was over, refreshed and clear-eyed, ready to go back into the cave. I liked going for a walk outside, feeling the air on my skin.

The articles and essays in this collection are gathered from these outings, featuring familiar yet extraordinary people captured at a significant moment of new art, new life or new love, sometimes approaching death; it adds a sadness and mystery to my meeting with Edwin Starr that he would die the following year. Other ghosts appear, of Michael Jackson, of Richard Yates with his scary houses and Jean Rhys with her infectious despair. There's a loose distinction I am making between the article and the essay: the former is mostly centred around an interview or is lighter in content; the latter is deeper, attempting to express a substantial idea or experience or a major impact someone has made on others. 'The aggressiveness of the essay is the assumption of the authority to speak in one's own voice,' wrote Elizabeth Hardwick.[1] And that is the point. The voice of non-fiction is visible, it takes the lead. In the personal essay, of which there are some here, the person behind the voice is also visible: the dancing self in 'Once a Dancer', the maternal self in 'How to

Tell the Children' or 'Travelling with my Daughter'. Strangely, this mode feels the closest to fiction while being its opposite. All writing is in some way a voyage of disappearance, a departure from the self outwards into the world.

In wanting to create a record of the beginning and development of the two voices, and how they have changed over the years, I have resisted the urge to interfere much with the earlier pieces, including dates and timelines. They show a young writer learning how to speak and take on muscle, while the overall period covered is another, partial record of our recent history (Grenfell, George Floyd, Covid). The right voice speaks at the right time and the other learns to step aside. I no longer feel I have to choose between them, or that they require different parts of the day. I have realised, finally, that it is possible to be both.

Diana Evans
London, 2024

Portraits

The Balcony

I am sitting in bed next to Mariah Carey. It's a sumptuous, nine-hundred-pounds-a-night king-size at the Landmark Hotel in London. Arranged supine, she flops one arm out in an exaggerated display of exhaustion at the toil involved in her 80 million record sales over seven years. 'I haven't stopped,' she says. 'I've put out more records than people who've been around twice as long as I have. Basically since right after high school I've been making records year after year after year.' She's wearing a pair of tiny boxer shorts and a belly-airing vest. I too am in my work clothes (black Miss Selfridge trousers, white Lycra top) holding at an angle a Sony voice recorder into which she will relate her recent crazy New York schedule completing her sixth album *Butterfly*, featuring Bone Thugs-n-Harmony. 'You can lie down if you want,' she says. 'I mean, it's fine, be comfortable.' So I lean further back into the pillows, feigning being comfortable.

Around six months earlier, an underemployed graduate in my mid-twenties, I had begun a two-week journalism internship at *Pride* magazine, a lifestyle glossy for women of colour containing beauty tips, news features, personality columns and coverage of arts and music. During my first week there, I'd sensed murky office tensions flying through the atmosphere, a gloominess, a pervasive, exploited disgruntlement. It was in the middle of my second week, by which time I had not yet learned the tenets of journalism, that the culture editor stormed out, and that evening I received a strange, unsettling phone call from the magazine's editor offering me the just-vacated post, which

involved flying to Nassau next Wednesday to cover a reggae festival. The salary was more than I had ever earned. I had a student
loan, an inchoate CV, lots of waitressing experience and no
other pending job offers. Terrified, I said yes.

The following Wednesday I was on a plane to the Bahamas
surrounded by movers and shakers of the Black-British press
standing in the aisles, leaning over each other's headrests, sip-
ping the complimentary drinks and gossiping about the festival
line-up or juicy industry news. I didn't know a soul except for
the photographer accompanying me to take pictures for my
pages. I tend to be shy in social situations. My usual strategy is
to act self-sufficient and thus disinterested, which can sometimes come across as rude: such as the next morning at the
swanky beach-hotel breakfast banquet when a friendly music
hack came up and introduced himself to me, and I exited the
conversation before it could start. I was worried about how I
was going to manage to interview Shaggy, Luciano, Sizzla and
Mutabaruka. Thanks to said friendly music hack, who succeeded in breaking through my veneer and went on to give me
some schooling on what questions to ask, how to open strong,
how to get them talking, I stumbled my way through it and
gathered enough material to fill my culture pages. I spent the
next two years covering music, movies, TV and books, attend-
ing a never-ending slew of album launches, film screenings and
press nights, and meeting a plethora of stars in various hotel
scenarios. Mariah was my first cover story.

'See this glitter on my nails?' she says, holding out her hands.
'I had eye make-up, like, *all* over my eyes and two sets of lashes.
It was, like, a showgirl theme, so I had all these snazzy little
outfits, but getting on a Concorde in daylight with gold make-
up on isn't really the look you wanna be sporting.' She's telling
me about the filming of the video for 'Breakdown', the Bone
Thugs-n-Harmony collaboration, which she co-directed, and

which is similar in costuming to the 'Honey' video where she is depicted imprisoned in a San Juan mansion wearing a slinky black chemise and a pair of Gucci stilettos that somehow she manages to run and swim in. When she's escaped her abductors by jumping out of the window into a conveniently positioned swimming pool, there is an underwater striptease ending in a skin-coloured bikini and the Guccis. 'Honey', the first single release off *Butterfly*, went straight in at No. 1 on the US *Billboard* Hot 100, and marked an apparent change in direction for Mariah, from sweet balladeer of weepers such as 'Hero' and 'I Don't Wanna Cry' to something edgier and sexier. 'I'm not Mary Poppins,' she says. 'A lot of people who meet me are, like, *Wow, you seem so different in person!* But even back to my first demos there was always an urban influence in my music. There were songs that should've been on a record but that didn't get on because everybody felt they were too progressive or too urban for where they wanted to take me. I won't just go and make a record and think that suddenly I've morphed into Lil' Kim or Foxy Brown.'

I wasn't a heavy Mariah Carey fan, but I used to listen to two of her songs on repeat, 'Fantasy' and 'Always Be My Baby', while walking along the Havana Malecón on a recent trip to Cuba, and I thought she sang with a most beautiful and affecting passion. I was mostly a reggae head. I liked Sanchez, Maxi Priest, Sizzla, Luciano (whom I was slightly in love with since seeing him live in Nassau where he'd appeared on stage topless, holding a staff, had knelt in the drift of the building background music and said, 'Let us pray'), Anthony B, Donna Marie, Judy Mowatt, Gregory Isaacs, Beres Hammond. I had the vinyl twelve inches of Tony Hearne's cover of 'Like Sister & Brother', 'Move Your Sexy Body' by The Administrators and Don Campbell's 'See It In Your Eyes', the kind of songs they used to play at the Apollo Nightclub in Willesden and during the reggae selection of Roundwood Park all-dayers. I also had a lot of British soul, funk and pop, such as Soul II Soul, The Brand New Heavies, The Pasadenas, Simply Red, Massive Attack and, from a teenage crush on Marti Pellow, Wet Wet Wet. Then there was the American hip-hop: A Tribe Called Quest (wasn't everyone in love with Q-Tip?), the Fugees, Public Enemy, Arrested Development, Tupac, De La Soul. Some soca, some West African highlife, jazz and Fela Kuti and Mary J. Blige, of course Prince, Earth, Wind & Fire, Madonna, Sam Cooke, Otis Redding, Tracy Chapman, Terry Callier and a little classical. Music was an accompaniment to the living of everyday life. I found it difficult to do anything without music, apart from sleeping and reading, and it was virtually impossible to get ready for a night out in silence. It was surely a dream job, then, to be sent copious amounts of CDs and be obliged to listen to them. At the time, I was living in a flat in Ladbroke Grove, having recently moved there from a shared house on the street where Bob Marley had recorded *Catch a Fire* and parts of *Exodus*. The friendly music hack had moved in with me. We took turns at a corner desk doing our transcriptions, went together to Janet Jackson's *The Velvet Rope* album launch at The Vaults in Waterloo and got the bus home afterwards.

The mid-to-late 1990s was an exciting time for black music. Hip-hop had become the biggest-selling genre on Earth, outselling rock and topping the mainstream pop charts on a regular basis. With the heady rise and heart-wrenching, bloody demise of Tupac Shakur and Biggie Smalls, a kind of biblical and tragic aura had attached itself to rap, alongside the ascending of new hardcore stars like Jay Z, No Limit and DMX whose tunes bass-thumped across the nightclub dancefloors, inside our Walkmans and from our three-tier hi-fi systems. It was when Puffy was not yet Diddy, when digital sampling from yesterday's rhythms became commonplace and we were first acquainted with what would become Beyoncé through the global espousal of Destiny's Child and hip-hop R&B. In reggae, the slump brought on by lyrical homophobia from the likes of Shabba Ranks and Buju Banton had given way to popular dancehall tracks from a new roster featuring Beenie Man and Sean Paul, plus Sizzla had arrived, with conscious yet militant love tracks like 'Black Woman & Child' and 'Dry Cry'. Meanwhile the UK was experiencing the homegrown explosion of garage, Craig David was on the horizon, the MOBO (Music of Black Origin) Awards was founded in 1996, while major labels were falling over themselves to sign Black-British talent like Glamma Kid, Mark Morrison and Shola Ama. Black music was now pop music – and Mariah Carey, who had been dubbed in some quarters the 'white Whitney' (she is half Venezuelan/African American and half Irish), was thought by some to be 'blacking up' her act with the *Butterfly* album in order to cash in on the shift in perspective on what was commercial. Actually, she was eager to highlight, she had already collaborated with the Wu Tang Clan's Ol' Dirty Bastard on *Fantasy*, so the presence of Puffy, Jermaine Dupri, Walter Afanasieff, The Ummah, Mase, The Trackmasters, Stevie J and Bone Thugs on the new album was not such a departure as people might think. 'Journalists say to me, All the black artists you've collaborated with on this album – how do you know them? Why do you only work with black artists? People will *say* stuff like that to me, and I'll then have to say, Well, first of all, my father is black, my mother is white, and therefore it's not such a big deal, and it's not like you should even be *asking* me this question!' One American journalist went so far as to complain, 'I hate it when people have a spit of black in them and they try to act like they're from the ghetto.' She splutters, 'If you want to critique my music or my clothes or my hair, that's fine, but don't try to tell me what my heritage is or how much black I have in me!"

We are interrupted by Mariah's personal assistant who places a cup of honey and lemon next to her on the bedside table. Every so often, she lets out a delicate cough. She tells me that she used to smoke but gave it up because she kept losing her voice. 'One time I was really afraid it wasn't gonna come back. And I prayed and I said if I get my voice back I'll never ever smoke again. Got it back, never smoked again.' I get the feeling, as Mariah Carey and I are talking – this is a common sensation when meeting celebrities – that I am a faceless being stripped of my particularities and personality and that she could be talking to anyone. But there is a contrasting notion that she wanted to be interviewed by this magazine specifically, to reach its readers, perhaps gain their sympathy, to adorn its cover as she would the coming February, wearing a black velvet fedora and a halter neck revealing a butterfly tattoo on her back. She talks a little about her pending divorce from Sony mogul Tommy Mottola. 'I didn't ever understand marriage – my parents got divorced when I was so young and I didn't have an example of a happy family.' She talks about her difficult childhood. 'Ever since then, I've had this mechanism of turning things off when they're unpleasant because that's how I got through everything.' Now, though, 'I feel like I'm in a good place. I feel like I'm getting back in touch with myself. I'm an emotional person, and music is like the emotional thread that I'm bound together by.' It's around then that the PA gives another, final reminder – 'Time's up!' – and we say goodbye. Mariah stretches luxuriantly, I get the Tube back to the office in Battersea.

Transcribing took hours. Every 'ah' and 'you know'. There was no digital dictation, hardly even an internet. We are talking battery-operated plastic tape recorders and fax machines. To do a telephone interview you would have to put a bulky plug in the wall and attach the tape recorder to your handset. We were using cassettes made of spools and that shiny brown magnetic tape wrapped around them. Sometimes the equipment mal-functioned and you might have to summarise memories of conversations. I knew of one journalist who reconstructed a whole article from recollections of entertaining gesticulation, which made up for the lack of quotes. It was a wild west of journalism where people stumbled into jobs because they happened to be in the right place at the right time, had late-night telephone conversations with members of the Fugees, flirty penthouse chats with Sisqo from Dru Hill. The stars were more accessible then, less gated and curated by their press teams and entourages, less media-trained, fan-thanking and ingratiating, which made for interesting copy and fewer manufactured quotes.

To write up my articles, I was using an essay-writing process left over from university, involving a plan and a quote-numbering system. There were some pieces where I got stuck because of boredom, which slowly turned into mental and spir-itual pain as I struggled to finish. I was not used to writing in this very public way, around a communal desk, with other people clattering at their keyboards. My first instinct towards any kind of literary form was in the solipsistic direction of poetry, and I found journalism creatively stifling. My sentences weren't allowed to be long enough. I liked more decoration and wordplay, to meander into unpredicted waters and hover in solitude. The reality of the situation, though, was that my hith-erto literary hovering had not produced much in terms of concrete matter, only a horde of earnest, disconnected scrib-blings and terrible poems. At least here I was producing complete segments of prose, which were being published. There were even some days when I would walk out of the *Pride* offices or out of an interview with someone mesmeric and transporting like Cassandra Wilson and feel that I was exactly where I wanted to be in the world.

The Black-British press was likewise thriving at that time, comprising a host of magazines and newspapers that had come into being as a response to the mainstream media routinely ignoring or misrepresenting black life and culture. The long-standing *The Voice* newspaper was rivalled by the *New Nation*; *Pride* had competitors in *Black Beauty & Hair* and *Woman II Woman* (a *Voice* supplement); on the music scene were *Touch* magazine, *Blues & Soul*, *Echoes*, *Mix Mag*, *Trace* and *True*, a kind of black equivalent to *Dazed & Confused*. These publications spawned an array of talented writers such as Darren Crosdale (who wrote the definitive Mark Morrison feature for *Touch*), Kevin le Gendre (one of the finest non-fiction writers this country has ever produced), Derek A. Bardowell, Jacqueline Springer, Afua Hirsh and Gemma Weekes. We were writing about the things that interested us in a way that was true, accurate, most of all *vital*, and undistorted by trope and stereotype. We were writing against invisibility, against white-centrism and mainstream negation, and many of us were there on that June summer's day at the Africa Centre in Covent Garden when Lauryn Hill was in town to promote her debut solo album, *The Miseducation of Lauryn Hill*, one of the most anticipated albums and solo career launches in hip-hop history. The press conference was full to the brim. She was eloquent, elegant and calm, in silver bangles, a powerful matte lipstick and a leather coat, her glossy black dreadlocks framing her face. Lauryn Hill was my second cover story.

'Listen, child,' she told me later that week in her dressing room. 'I'm one of those old young people – I feel forty and I'm only twenty-three.' Her eyes were twinkling slits. She was in her first year of motherhood. A national TV star by the age of fifteen, as lead vocalist of the Fugees Hill had already seen multi-platinum album success with *The Score*. Chuck D had dubbed her 'the Bob Marley of the twenty-first century', the world was bopping to 'Doo Wop', and this time she was on her own – no Wyclef, no Pras. 'If you don't deliver or produce, it's all your fault,' she said. 'You can't blame anyone else.'

We were sitting on high stools. Today she was wearing a sweatshirt with faded jeans and a pair of platforms. That morning on my way to work I had collided with a bicycle while running for my bus and was still a little headspun, but I didn't feel I could tell Lauryn Hill this unless it came up in a conversation, which it didn't. The basic dynamic of the journalistic interview is that the interviewer reveals nothing about themselves while the interviewee is encouraged to reveal everything. If it had a comparable object, it would be a funnel.

By now I'd drawn up a list of questions to ask celebrities: What is your first memory? Describe the house you grew up in. What is your favourite possession? What is the most important thing to remember in moments of uncertainty? What animal were you in your past life?, to which Lionel Richie answered, over the phone, that he was a bird, which seemed somehow accurate. I'd also learned that flattery is useful. Somewhere near the beginning of the interview, I would deliver some flattery of the album, book or movie that had enabled me to meet this person, and with Lauryn it was a privilege to offer my personal appreciation of *Miseducation*, the rawness of its guitar chords, the brilliance of the beats on 'Lost Ones', the massage to the heart and ear of her rich, muscled and mellow voice.

'Stuff just sort of spilled out,' she said. 'I was able to be in my own head for a moment. I'm not embarrassed to show that I'm vulnerable on a record, because that's the tradition of music that I was raised in. I make music less for perfection and more for emotion.' It showed. Entirely self-produced, she revealed that there were raised eyebrows at her decision to make the album alone, even though she had by this time produced songs for Aretha Franklin and CeCe Winans. 'We live in a sexist world. People never ask men questions when they choose to self-produce or write anything. But when a woman decides to take charge of her project, people get a little sceptical.' She was similarly miffed about the tendency in the music industry to prioritise making lucrative hits over artistic substance. 'You have performers out there who spend more time marketing themselves than making music, so of course the music is gonna suffer.'

Now she was standing, her arms supporting her on the stool as if she had a bad back, or maybe her shoes were hurting. Every so often she would clop around a bit, still talking: ' hip-hop. It's like that. It's kinda like a folk music that's for young people and common people who keep it alive, you know. And every time the establishment thinks it's created something different and got its hands around it, it changes, and it changes so quickly.'

Meanwhile her son Zion was waiting at home in South Orange, New Jersey, for his mother's loving arms. There had been some anxiety in naming him thus. Was it too heavy a name to place on a baby? Would it become a burden to him in the future? But no other name quite fit. 'When I think of Zion, I think of the saviour, the salvation, a heavenly place. And he's definitely been my safe place, my salvation from humbler times. My relationships outside of the music industry are so precious to me now. I never want to neglect my family.'

Rohan Marley, Zion's father and son of Bob, was waiting for her in South Orange as well, and whatever happened over the following years and four more kids, she smiled when she spoke of him, of how he'd won her heart. 'For the first time, I didn't have to carry someone. Nor was I made to feel bad for who I was. He took care of me. "Lauryn, how are you? Hey, are you eating? What did you have for breakfast?" He was one of those phone calls, one of those people who was genuinely concerned about my well-being.'

There were other cover stories, other conversations. I met girl bands and boy bands, neo soul singers and what felt like a hundred rappers. Despite my love of music, despite the supposed privilege of receiving sacks of free CDs, I eventually began to see that there is only so long you can go on listening to R&B singers talking very similarly about the inspiration behind their love songs, or the break-out rhymer's arrival at their beats. After two years, the mental and spiritual pain of those difficult articles was deepening and it was taking longer to get past the blocks. I knew it was time to move on when my telephone interview with Luther Vandross was cut short by his perception of my boredom and my perception of his reluctance to be interviewed. Neither of us could pretend anymore. The funnel collapsed. I followed my predecessor out the door, and drifted into the freelance pool of photographers, would-be poets, aspiring writers and underpaid journalists, observing and rendering the culture as we saw it. I do believe on some profound level that my natural place as a scribe is on the balcony overlooking the spectacle with my fellow observers, the glow of the night lights giving a special kind of access, the distance from the ground expanding our perception of what's at the centre. I belong in that shadowy outer room, set away from the thoroughfare, so that I can see everything clearly. There is community there, one of excitement, intellect and warmth: the outer side of solipsism.

Earth Calling Wilson

A limp, copper light wafts over a darkened auditorium. The musicians are perched quietly at their instruments, fingers laid lightly on piano keys, sticks for beats in hand, waiting. Even before the feathery entrance of their tranquil, modest 'leader', there is an atmosphere of serenity. Then, when the silence itself has become a kind of overture, Cassandra Wilson treads slowly on stage in a deceptively transparent pink nightie, looking something like a nostalgic flower-power hippie from Mississippi. She could've just that minute before fallen out of bed. Heavy lids and sleepy leans every which way, there's nevertheless a confident nonchalance, reassuring the already mesmerised audience that she will eventually sing. When she opens her mouth, there it is. The pitch-black, deep and haunting voice commanding folk- and blues-flecked jazz accompaniments to walk with its spirit. This voice and transgressive sensibility have confirmed Cassandra Wilson as one of the greatest female jazz vocalists and composers of her time.

'I can go into a zone anywhere, anyplace, anytime.' Wilson speaks like she sings. Long pauses of premeditation, words and syllables dancing randomly down like balloons to the tip of her Southern tongue. Her 'zones' can be difficult places to get to, especially for spectators used to the more conventional features of live performance, such as immediate connection with the audience and a domineering leadership presence. This rustic figure, copper-crowned with thick, heavy locks, often seems so self-absorbed, almost sloppy on stage, there's sometimes a worry that the whole thing might fall apart. In fact, it's as clammy and stuck together as wet earth. 'I'd describe it more as trance,' she says. 'It's really a releasing of the ego. My approach has always been to come to the stage not as the leader, or not as the star, but more as the main participant in a ritual, because I believe that the performance of this music is more ritual than entertainment.' The audience, she adds, is not considered 'as being outside of myself'.

A mature, quiet woman with a musky presence and a lazy white smile, Wilson's individualistic interpretation of her genre at first annoyed many a jazz purist. Bringing in the influences of pop, rock and folk could easily be misconstrued as an incongruous meeting of the 'authentic' and the commercial that even Cassandra herself was once nervous of. Artists as diverse as U2, The Monkees, Joni Mitchell, Van Morrison and country icon Hank Williams have all found their way into the tissues of her sound, and in the same way that Nina Simone and Billie Holiday electrified their generation with vocals and lyricism that seemed blessed, Cassandra Wilson eventually began to shine within the jazz world as well as receive credibility on the commercial stage. Despite the seven albums she'd accomplished beforehand, it wasn't until her first recording with Blue Note, *Blue Light 'til Dawn* (1993), that she gained international recognition. The album sold in excess of 250,000 copies worldwide, making it one of the top-selling jazz records of the year. The following Grammy Award-winning album, *New Moon Daughter* (1995), was no less piercing, and she even had the nerve to open it with a cover of Billie Holiday's excoriating evocation of black lynching, 'Strange Fruit'. Definitely, with her mournful contralto tone and wayward pacing, she's the only person who could do it without sounding too pretty and losing the bitter sense of horror.

'It's been this way from the beginning,' Wilson explains. 'When I first began my career, I was labelled unpredictable. So

no one is really surprised now when I take these excursions.'
This time it's Miles Davis. And her intention to interpret his
legendary music on her thirteenth album, *Travelling Miles* (which
was originally conceived as a concert for the Lincoln Center in
New York) did set some tongues wagging. She describes it as 'a
tribute, an offering to the spirit of Miles Davis'. Her decision to
embark on such a tall order reflects her own observation that
she's found more confidence in herself as a musician and as a
writer, 'and particularly with this project, as a producer'. Produced by Wilson and featuring Nigerian Afro-funk artist
Angelique Kidjo, the album presents a high-flying collection of
characteristically unpredictable renditions (such as Cindy Lau-
per's 'Time After Time') and amiable nods to folk and pop,
while staying in a kind of celestial tune with Davis's tendencies
of adventure, transcendent beauty and experimentation. Distant plucks on a Spanish guitar, fleeting Latin chords and the
bassy warmth of African drums flaunt a new global emphasis
treasured by a woman whose mother, she relates, used to call her
a gypsy. 'It's about travelling on different levels,' she says. 'It's
about exchange. In jazz we look at the music as a vehicle, it's a
way to access other cultures, to move around the world as jazz
musicians, to share this music with people . . . And that's been
my approach to "jazz" music – overall it's about inclusivity. We
know what the fundamental basis of the music is, where it
comes from, how it has evolved into what it is today, and we're
sort of the caretakers of that music. And I believe that it's really
important, it's our responsibility, to push it forward.' Nowadays
she calls herself 'a professional gypsy'.

Hailing from Jackson, Mississippi, Cassandra Wilson grew up
the only daughter of a Chicago-born jazz guitarist and bassist,
Herman Fowlkes, and a Southern school teacher, Mary McDan-
iel. She and her three brothers practically lived outdoors, coming

in from nature to eat and sleep in a household warmed by jazz, folk, Motown and her grandmother's steaming herbal medicines. 'Let me just say this,' she tells me when I ask to hear more about these concoctions, 'I believe in 'erbs. I believe in the use of all kinds of 'erbs; plantlife is really important.' At the age of nine, she began studying classical piano and was writing songs on guitar by the time she was twelve. Her father being a follower of the Bahá'í Faith, she was inspired by its doctrine that humankind is one, God is one and all religions are one. He died a few years back, the same year that *Blue Light 'til Dawn* was born. 'Death is part of a cycle – it's not the end,' she says. 'It's really a triumph, in a sense, moving from one plane to the next. We seem to go, but I don't think we ever go anywhere. You have ancestors who are there and, you know, just kinda hanging out, and you may have brought a part of their spirits into your earthly incarnation.' It certainly seems that way in her presence, that Wilson is connected to other planes of being, a higher or deeper consciousness that lifts her from the mundane and feeds into her music.

When she was nineteen she began travelling around Mississippi and Arkansas performing folk guitar and vocals, the everywhere blues arresting her senses – that's when her mother started calling her a gypsy. After fetching a degree in Mass Communication at Jackson State University, she moved to New Orleans and worked in television as an assistant public-affairs director. It was on meeting an early mentor, saxophonist Earl Turbinton, and then relocating to New York with her first husband, where she was unable to get another job in television, that Wilson immersed herself in making jazz. She made her first recordings as a singer with a jazz/hip-hop outfit called M-Base, until *Blue Light 'til Dawn* inscribed her name on international soil. She now has a son, Jeris, and lives and works in a Harlem apartment previously inhabited by Duke Ellington. Engaged again, this time to a French actor of Ivory Coast roots whom she calls her 'prince', she reveals a quiet doubt about the forthcoming marriage, embarrassed that this relationship of two years is the longest she's had. 'There's a lot of anxiety connected to the idea of marriage – how things change when you make that commitment in public . . . But looking back I understand why those last two marriages weren't successful, and that I can't bring the baggage from those old relationships into this one.'

Wilson's great-grandmother was born into slavery. In the spirit of a civil-rights movement that yearned for a familiar African identity while challenging oppression in a forcibly assigned 'home', and of a black womanist movement that yearned for female liberation within a racially cognisant framework, she has used her music to address profound questions about the human condition. To her, it's a universal as well as personal therapy for the common experience of struggle. 'The oppression that I've experienced as a woman is very closely tied to the oppression that I've experienced as a black person,' she says. 'So the issues that I address in my music concerning both racial and sexual discrimination pretty much parallel each other. It's about dealing with the reasons why we have these problems in our society, why at this point in humanity, where we should be truly evolved as a species, we are still having to deal with these outdated notions of womanhood, of what it means to be non-white. We're still grappling with these issues, and I think the key to our success is to confront them, you know, and to heal ourselves.' And language is a crucial element in this. As an incarcerated Malcolm X once pored sourly over the English dictionary, Cassandra Wilson looks into her consciousness to find a colonialism-stained vocabulary that she can only turn around in order to do herself justice. 'Darkness has become richness for me. I love to play with the idea of darkness as being positive, black as positive as opposed to what we deal with in our language . . . What if darkness is something that's wonderful and tranquil and peaceful and beautiful? What if you use the word "sweet" and "black" at the same time?'

I left her dancing to a distant piano wafting in with the daylight. The dreaming gypsy whirling in new love, new music, new possibility, in her perpetual trance she travels. Cassandra Wilson is Alice Walker's definition of womanist: 'Loves music. Loves dance. Loves the moon. *Loves* the spirit. Loves love and food and roundness. Loves struggle. *Loves* the folk. Loves herself. Regardless.' Long may she roam.

Pride, 1999

Carlos Acosta: The World at His Feet

When he was a boy, breakdancing and loitering in the streets of Havana, Carlos Acosta never considered ballet as a way out of poverty. Ballet was an art for the elite; it was fairyland on tiptoes, and real life was lived in a tiny flat in the neighbourhood of Los Pinos, where Coke cans lined the living-room walls in place of pictures. This is why, twenty years after his truck-driver father sent him to ballet school for discipline and free food, Acosta still thinks of what has happened in his life as a miracle.

These days he's regarded as one of the greatest classical dancers in the world, with comparisons often made to Rudolf Nureyev and Mikhail Baryshnikov. A vast skyward jump, dizzying pirouettes and a warm and formidable stage presence earned him early principal status at the English National Ballet (ENB) at the age of eighteen. At the time of writing he's a regular star attraction for the Houston Ballet, American Ballet Theatre and – as guest principal since 1998 – with The Royal Ballet in Covent Garden. Recently, for the Opera Bastille in Paris, he guest-danced the title role in Nureyev's *Don Quixote*, which is widely considered the ultimate technical challenge for a ballet dancer.

Allen Robertson, the editor of *Dance Now* magazine and dance editor of *Time Out*, first saw Acosta perform in the ENB, when Acosta was nineteen. 'Even then it was clear that he has an extra dimension to him,' Robertson remembers. 'His technique is everything that technique should be, but at the same time it is full of his own kind of power and masculine grace. He manages to be both dynamic and correct, and it's obvious, no matter what role you're seeing him dance, that he loves to be on stage. One really important thing about the way Acosta performs is that he doesn't ever diminish the choreography he's dancing – he doesn't dance 'I'm the star'. He's certainly one of the shining lights of his generation.'

Last year, he turned his hand to choreography with his dance theatre production *Tocororo – A Cuban Tale*, a sassy mélange of Afro-Cuban and classical dance exploring the conflicts of leaving home, which gets its second run at Sadler's Wells in London this summer. Aside from its big-hearted theatricality, *Tocororo* (the name of the national bird of Cuba) is also a reflection of the conflicts that exist in Acosta's life. The visceral flamboyance of Afro-Cuban culture tussles with the linearity and elitism of ballet; a young man leaves behind the familiarity of home for the challenges and glitter of the unknown.

'When I was a child,' the dancer explains, fresh from a morning rehearsal; we are drinking coffee in the offices of the Royal Opera House, 'I didn't know anything about ballet. We were not educated people in my family; we didn't really have any aspirations. You could say that we lived on the other side of ballet.'

Like many performing artists of Acosta's stature, he looks a lot smaller up close than he does on stage. He has bright, candid eyes and a jagged fringe of tight black curls, and these boyish looks are something of a contrast to the gruff accent and rigid handshake. Acosta is someone for whom busyness is a constant. He gives off the impression that everything must be done quickly. As well as leading a thriving dance career and a fledgling choreographic one, he is also, at the age of thirty-one, penning his autobiography. In an age of premature memoir, it may well stand out as one that's actually worth reading, not just as a story of personal achievement but as an insight into one of the most compelling cultures in the world. 'Like many Cubans,' he says, 'I grew up with Afro-Cuban culture as a big part of my life. Cuba is composed of lots of different races, and you could say that the most dominant of these is African. My father was a follower of the religion of Santeria. He had a sanctuary in the living room, so it was a prominent part of our lives. Santeria is synonymous with Cuba: those Afro-Cuban rhythms, the rumba, even the salsa – that's where it all comes from.'

Santeria evolved in Cuba from the ancient Yoruba worship of the Orishas, the Yoruba gods, transported to the Caribbean through slavery. Incorporating elements of Catholicism (an attempt to disguise the forbidden practice of native worship from enslavers), the religion permeates Afro-Cuban dance and music. Each Orisha has its own character dance – the ferocious stomp of Shango the god of thunder; the sensuous, watery sway of Oshun the divinity of love – and Acosta includes some of these dances in *Tocororo*. 'It was important for me to put these elements into my show, because that is where my roots are, even though ballet is the career I pursued.'

The Afro-Cuban style of movement could not be further removed from ballet. 'They're totally different techniques and flavours,' Acosta explains. 'Classical dance is very strict, and you need to have a certain kind of body and a certain kind of training. On the contrary, the Afro-Cuban is really a kind of street dance. One of the things I regret is not learning it well enough. But when you are a classical dancer, that's all you do, Tchaikovsky and all those guys.' In a demonstration of the Afro-Cuban style, he starts moving around in his chair, throwing his arms and legs outwards and smirking. 'It's all about the attitude, you know; you have to project much more of it. Whereas ballet is about poise and beauty.'

Taking up the reins of choreography is an ambitious move for a dancer, and it's not always successful. Dancers are accustomed to offering their bodies as canvas for choreography; it's another thing altogether to become the dance-maker, to deal with all the considerations of space and pace and musicality and theatrical cohesion that make a dance work. *Tocororo*, last year, was like a good first novel; promising in its language and passion, yet clattering in places over awkward joins and scenes not quite brought to fullness. In a schedule involving some eight hours of dancing a day and frequent gigs abroad, Acosta will have twenty days left in which to make improvements. 'I want to create new scenes and try to link it in a way that it flows better,' he says.

As we speak, the *Tocororo* cast is rehearsing in Cuba without him. This includes seventeen dancers from a combination of the Cuban National Ballet, the Conjuncto Folklórico Nacional (which specialises in the Afro-Cuban dances) and Danza Contemporanea, as well as Acosta's fourteen-year-old nephew Yonah Acosta, who plays the protagonist in his childhood. Although Acosta is mindful of the fact that there's work to be done, he makes no claims to any exceptional aptitude for choreography. 'I don't really see myself as a choreographer. Choreographers, like Balanchine and all those guys who made lots of massive pieces, are geniuses, and I don't try to compete with them. I just want to create a show that people can relate to, to say things that haven't been said before.'

There is an inclination in *Tocororo* towards bridging the gap between elitist art forms and those that emerge on the street, out of particular social and cultural circumstances. Acosta's background gives him a unique perspective on what art should do, what dance should do, and he is dubious about the concept of 'art for art's sake'. 'There are a lot of artists doing surreal things with dance, like with computer technology, but it's all very surreal. It doesn't give you a message, it doesn't make you dream, it doesn't tell a story. That's what I'm trying to do. I want to bring Afro-Cuban dance and hip-hop and salsa and such arts to the main stage, where you'd usually see the classics – and do it with quality, so that it fits. We live in a world of fusion, and I think we should try to achieve that in ballet as well.'

The Havana flat in which Acosta, the youngest of eleven children, was brought up was a crowded, makeshift place with one bedroom. 'There was a very small bathroom with a big tank of water. We had real problems with water. We had to carry it bucket by bucket from the downstairs hallway every day. Most of the time we were about eight people living there, but at some point my mother's family moved in with us because they were in exile and waiting for their papers. They were two aunts, my grandmother and my cousin, and at that time there was twelve of us.' Acosta's first experiences in dance were as a pint-size breakdancer, competing against rival gangs when he was nine. But this had less to do with any burning desire to be a dancer than with wanting to bunk off school. 'I just liked to go with the flow. I realised that I could skip classes for two months and then just go back to school and it wouldn't matter that much.'

He was not a particularly ambitious child. If there was anything he harboured a passion for, it was that universal boyhood dream of becoming a footballer. Acosta's father, though, envisaged the future Carlos as more of a delinquent – the truancy, the stealing from shops – and he heard about some neighbours who had sent their child to ballet school and got them off the streets (the meals were free too). Acosta hated ballet school; he was kicked out twice for misbehaving. It was not until he saw the Cuban National Ballet perform live, when he was thirteen, that he began to change his mind. 'I saw the professionals doing all those jumps and leaps and I was really impressed. It was from that point that I started to work hard.'

This new shift in attitude revealed to Acosta's teachers a

particular talent for ballet that had until then been hidden by
sloth and lack of ambition. 'They saw my potential and began
choreographing for me. It was a good feeling to be wanted like
that, to feel important. It was a new feeling for me, you know,
and I liked it. I could see then that I could produce something
worthwhile when I dance that would have an impact on people.'
The whirlwind that Acosta's career turned into gathered pace,
and in 1990 the sixteen-year-old prodigy scooped the gold medal
at the Prix de Lausanne, the world's most significant international student ballet award. It was the first of many awards,
and Acosta's international credits clocked up rapidly. Travelling
the world may only ever be a dream for many ordinary Cubans,
often restricted from spontaneously crossing their country's
borders, but the teenage Acosta was making regular trips to
Europe, South America and beyond.

'Sometimes you need a miracle,' he says, 'and that's what
happened to me, because I never expected anything. I never
expected to be sitting here talking in another language, travelling the world and all these things. In Cuba, when you're poor,
you work hard and you go with the flow; you don't know what
the future holds or what to expect, and sometimes talent alone
is not enough. There's a very fine line between success and
failing – just one event can put you off course and make you lose
your focus.'

By the time he joined the Royal Ballet as its first black male
principal, Acosta was in a position to make a firm stand against
any hint of novelty treatment or exoticism. 'I've always been
conscious that they didn't typecast me, that I had an equal
amount of opportunities as everybody else, because I knew I
could dance any role out there. At the beginning they were testing me, watching me, because although I already had worldwide
recognition, it still doesn't mean anything until they've put you
on trial.'

Cuba's strict fostering of its ballet has produced some great dancers, among them Andres Williams and Fernando Bujones, two giants of the American scene. *Tocororo* features another rising star, José Oduardo Perez, who takes Acosta's role in six of the Sadler's Wells shows. Allen Robertson cites a particular fearlessness as the magic that makes Cuban dancers special. 'Even though they are perfectly trained and their technique is very honed, they just don't hold back. They go for broke. Carlos goes for broke, and that's what makes him such an exciting dancer.' Ballet training in Cuba is funded by the government and taught in a rigid manner, similar to the Russian style. The outcome is an instantly recognisable national technique, big on physique, athleticism and suspension, and certainly in some ways attributable to Cuba's prevailing atmosphere of austerity.

Lazaro Carreño, a principal teacher at the Houston Ballet, is a former colleague and teacher of Acosta's and a pioneer of dance training in Cuba. 'I was hired to teach in Cuba in the 1970s,' Carreño says. 'I'd studied in Leningrad and around the world, and I selected the best teaching techniques from the world's schools and integrated these into my methods. That first generation I taught produced a male dancing revolution, and every year the dancers improved.'

Acosta may feed off a perpetual sense of amazement at his good fortune, but this is perhaps not to be mistaken for happiness. A recent BBC documentary shadowed him through the making of *Tocororo* and its premiere in Cuba before an audience containing Fidel Castro. The film depicted a brooding character with an eternal frown. He seemed constantly harassed by a feverish schedule, utterly homesick and isolated by the demands of stardom. It was only in the Cuban scenes, passing time in Havana with old friends and family, that Acosta seemed to relax. The picture was not entirely accurate, he says. 'I am not a sad man, but happiness doesn't sell, you know. Who cares about happiness? And it's true, it was a very hard time for me, and it shows the tiredness and moodiness perhaps too much. But I think they were also trying to show that dancing is not an easy life. We work extremely hard and we pay a price. People don't often see that side of it.'

The central message in *Tocororo* is simple and, for Acosta, very personal: there is something lost in anything gained. He has good friends in Britain; his north London flat, where he lives alone, is a home from home; and he has work that feels like flying. But he would give everything up for one thing: 'To have my family around me. Family is the centre of life and there is no point in having things if you can't share them with those you love. I'm much happier when I'm in Cuba.'

Independent, 2004

Edwin Starr in Basingstoke

Into the purple stage-lights of Basingstoke's The Anvil theatre walk three ambassadors of the Motown legacy. Freda Payne (singer of the 1970 hit 'Band of Gold'), now in her fifties, has shimmied her firm thighs into a pair of gold hot pants. Martha Reeves (lead singer of Martha & the Vandellas) has on a white suit with a single violet button on the bodice. And Edwin Starr, deliverer of the twentieth century's most famous anti-military song 'War', stands between them. They are the darlings of this year's Dancing in the Streets tour, which runs across the UK. Behind them their backing singers two-step in tight black suits with silver streaks down the shoulders. Behind them all are blown-up photographs of an adolescent Stevie Wonder, and the iconic façade of Hitsville U.S.A., the birthplace studios and headquarters of Motown in Detroit, Michigan.

Starr's hair is glittering and he doesn't move about much in his loose black tuxedo. 'This isn't my show,' he told me not an hour before, backstage in his dressing room, sitting next to his Diet Coke in a cute blue tracksuit and little white pumps (it doesn't take him long to get ready – he's been doing this for forty-five years). 'In *my* show, we don't play around! It's about getting down from the moment you walk on stage to the moment you come off.' Edwin Starr and his band have been Northern soul's number-one live act for the past decade. Born Charles Edwin Starr in Tennessee in 1942 and raised in Ohio, he moved across the Atlantic to the West Midlands seventeen years ago in search of a public who still had a taste for the up-tempo, feel-good soul famously monopolised by Berry Gordy's Motown label. The US scene was drying up, rock music was taking over, 'and there were a lot of artists, like myself,' Starr explains, 'who just didn't want to be a part of it. It would mean becoming someone you didn't want to be.'

Luckily, punters up and down the UK wanted Starr just the way he was. His gorgeous, rough-edged voice (which sounds as good as ever – it is a paradigm of preservation). His great warm presence and gift for invoking the notion to dance wildly in flared trousers with buttons all the way up the ribcage. Northern soul blew up in the nightclubs of North England and the Midlands during the 1960s and spread across the country, reaching its peak in the mid-1970s, though it is still alive and well today, is even undergoing something of a resurgence. The Motown sound that was losing its commercial foundation in the US was contrarily hunted and demanded across the waters. Landmark Northern soul clubs like The Twisted Wheel in Manchester, The Blackpool Mecca and, perhaps the biggest of all, The Wigan Casino were thumping with songs from The Temptations, The Supremes and The Four Tops, alongside lesser-known artists whose songs were only released in limited numbers, part of the genre's custom of embracing what lies at the fringes of the music landscape. Born to a large extent out of the British mod scene, Northern soul became a kind of cult subculture, shunned by the mainstream, exclusive, enigmatic, and the artists were its feted leaders.

'The US is predicated on the newest, the biggest and the brightest – they have no allegiance to anything,' reflects Starr. 'But Europe, especially England, is built on nostalgia. You covet and love things that are old. Northern soul is a music of memories.' He still gets to smiling when he thinks back to the genesis of 'War'. Originally a Temptations song, and Edwin already having the 1969 hit, '25 Miles', under his belt, he was asked to take the mic for the riskiest project Motown had ever

attempted. An anti-war song, in the midst of Vietnam? 'They
knew it was a good record but they also knew that it was political dynamite and could've gone completely the opposite way,'
he explains, himself a former US military draftee. But 'War'
made gold before the label had even advertised it and spent three
weeks at number one on the *Billboard* Hot 100 in 1970. The song
is immortal, more famous than Starr himself. It pops up in
action movies like *Rush Hour* and kids' flicks like *Small Soldiers*,
and when Starr does his Butlin's and Pontins gigs the front row
is a line of munchkins waiting for him to sing that song – he
never gets tired of it.

There were other hits, such as 'Contact', 'H.A.P.P.Y. Radio'
and 'Agent Double-O-Soul', which have likewise blasted from
speakers across the world for the last three or four decades and
kept Starr singing into his sixties. He's so busy, what with Liza
Minnelli's wedding ('*everybody* was there') and the Jackson Five
reunion concert in New York, he can't even remember how he
celebrated his sixtieth birthday in January. 'This is what I do,' he
says fondly. 'I walk, talk, sleep, eat and breathe entertainment.
At this age I never thought I'd even be alive, let alone making
music! But luckily, God's got another plan for me. So I'm here.
I'm working, I'm happy, I'm fine. And I'm at a wonderful place
in my career where I don't have to prove anything to anybody.'
He can wear tracksuits in interviews and pumps without socks.
He can reel off stories about Jimi Hendrix ('we all used to meet
up after gigs and stuff – he was a nice guy, one of those freaks of
nature'). And there still exist places on Earth that Edwin Starr
can walk into and not be recognised – until he's on stage. 'I'm
fortunate in that I've never had an image I have to live up to –
my songs have carried me through. That to me is the best way to
be an artist.'

When asked for his thoughts on contemporary soul music,
Starr is noncommittal. The Jill Scotts and Erykah Badus, the

D'Angelos and Alicia Keyses of this world may be clinching multiple Grammys and making their own history, but to Starr they have a long way to go. 'Artists today believe they're superstars before they've even got a record out,' he says emphatically. 'That's why they're here today and gone tomorrow, because you can't teach them anything. They're not following in our footsteps; they're treading on them.' If he had the power, then, and if indeed these fledglings were to seek his advice, what of Motown would he inject into contemporary music? 'Nothing,' he replies. 'Absolutely nothing.'

Fashionline, 2002

Michael Jackson: On the Wall

At first, the artist Kehinde Wiley didn't believe it was Michael Jackson calling so he didn't pick up. 'Will you please answer the fucking phone?' a mutual friend said. And sure enough, not long afterwards, a meeting was set up and Wiley and Jackson were chewing the fat on such things as the function of clothes as body armour and the distinctions between Peter Paul Rubens's earlier and later brushwork. The resulting painting (*Equestrian Portrait of King Philip II*), completed after Jackson's death in 2009, shows a magnificent Michael in full armour on an ivory horse, flanked by multicultural cherubim and vivid roses in a distant barren land, rain clouds overhead. The look on his face is hard, determined, haughty, with a hint of vulnerability underneath.

It was Michael Jackson's astronomical celebrity that made Wiley think the call was a prank – a fame that is central to the National Portrait Gallery's exhibition of contemporary art inspired by Jackson's image and work. Titled with a pun after, arguably, his best album (though some say *Thriller*, others *Bad*), *Michael Jackson: On The Wall* gathers together the work of forty-eight disparate artists exploring the legacy of perhaps the most frequently depicted cultural figure in history, and his fame is their common palette. He is inseparable from it. It was his making and his tragedy. It glows with a bright, mournful edge from each one of these exhibits, probing the question of what might have been if his enormous success had not in some way required, or at least contributed to, his eventual annihilation.

Wiley's sumptuous portrait, displayed here for the first time in the UK, is mounted against a recurring blood-red back-ground, adjacent to a contrasting work by Lyle Ashton Harris, *Black Ebony II* (2010), a painting on Ghanaian funerary fabric of Jackson on the cover of *Ebony* magazine in 2007. While Harris's approach examines the confluence of modern globalisation and African cultural tradition amidst the hauntings of colonial tyr-anny, Wiley's work is known for presenting contemporary black figures (Barack Obama among them) in the visual lan-guage of European art history, thereby disrupting stereotypical perceptions of black identity and representation. There is a sense, in both portraits, of Michael Jackson as a site of supreme existential determinism, imprisoned by his image – its politics, its metamorphosis, its discomfort – yet uncompromis-ing in his idiosyncrasy.

Certainly during my childhood I was aware that there was no one else quite like Michael Jackson. I liked his leathers and his strut, his riveting shrieks and the white suit in the *Smooth Criminal* video. Most of all it was the deep high soulfulness in his music, it was a sound that seemed to unify all others. And then of course, no one else could move like him, with that almost superhuman, logic-defying agility. He was a captivating demonstration of how the body can best make use of music, and one of the pleasures of this show is its natural sonic dimension.

At the entrance is Donald Urquhart's *A Michael Jackson Alpha-bet* (2017), recalling the Jackson 5 song 'ABC', a vast, jumping display of buzzwords, 'D is for Dance!', 'T is for *Thriller*' going on all the way to 'Z is for Zombies'. Simultaneously there is music itself, wafting out from the blood-red rooms, that unmis-takable, honey-toned voice and a Quincy Jones backing track. You walk into a windswept dance move, a digital vision in four parts of Michael in motion, composed of stills from his 1987 short film *The Way You Make Me Feel*, rendered here under the same title by the installation artist Dara Birnbaum. In one still image, Jackson's sharp little chin and nose point upwards into blue mist; in another, the boyish hips are jutted, the hands arranged above the head like a bird in flight, beautifully capturing the ethereal lightness of his movements.

There are so many Michaels here, abstract and explicit, symbolic and personal, among the most striking the majestic, biblically themed photographic portraits of David LaChapelle, thick with drama and fantastic weirdness. LaChapelle began his career working for Andy Warhol (whose 1984 blue-flecked rendition of the icon also appears in this show), and his large-scale series 'American Jesus' depicts Jackson as a kind of funky, modern-day saint, shrouded in religious iconography and a rich, slightly saccharine naturalism. In *The Beautification: I'll Never Let You Part For You're Always In My Heart* (2009), Michael is gaunt and ghostly, his stage clothes loose around his frame and unspectacular next to the lush-veiled angel by his side, her holy hand resting lightly in his, a navy ocean at their backs. It has a feel of the world having ended, with Michael perhaps the only one saved, after a lifetime of crucifixion. In *American Jesus: Hold Me, Carry Me Boldly* (2009), the picture is less hopeful, less redemptive, with Michael splayed dead in the arms of a possible, heavenward-looking Jesus.

In almost every portrait, Jackson's eyes are striking – staring, testing or withholding – and a section of the exhibition is dedicated to them. They are headboard-studded in Isaac Lythgoe's surreal *The Only Here Is Where I Am* (2016), just the eyes, defaced and disembodied, yet recognisable. In Gary Hume's characteristically spare and graphic high-gloss painting, simply titled *Michael* (2001), their clear sadness is highlighted by chunky black brows and the frightened red lips, that deathly white complexion, drawn from the classic image of the man at perhaps his most outwardly vulnerable. Meanwhile in this section there is footage playing in a dark annex of the Bucharest leg of Jackson's

1992 *Dangerous* tour, shortly after the fall of communism and the collapse of the Eastern bloc. Crazed fans scream at a turn of his head, a flick of his hand. Even a suggestion of the removal of his sunglasses causes fainting and fits of crying. The masks that were handed out for free at this concert are arranged in an eye-level row surrounding, also watching the screen, their empty pupils replaced by electric lights. The recurring theme throughout is of Michael Jackson as a godlike figure, existent among us though imbued with the divine, visible yet unreachable, with the music the cord that connected him to us.

The show would not be complete without Bubbles, who for a time was the world's most famous chimp, or Jackson's close friend Elizabeth Taylor, or that leather dinner jacket with the cutlery hanging off it that used to make people laugh, all of which are present in various guises. But the more interesting work is that which illuminates Michael Jackson not as eccentric celebrity, but as a human being with specific cultural significance globally, such as Njideka Akunyili Crosby's collages of a Nigerian home, *As We See You: Dreams of Jand* (2017), and Todd Gray's seductive yet elusive layered photographs that replace Michael's head with another image, resisting binary interpretation. Jackson signifies many things, a pair of dancing shoes and a bouquet of balloons, a cluster of microphones, as in David Hammons's *Which Mike do you want to be like . . . ?* (2001), yet his essence remains as mysterious and private as our deepest selves. He was an expression of blackness and of sheer, freewheeling individuality at the same time.

This is what the last piece in the exhibition seems to point to, Candice Breitz's video montage *King (A Portrait of Michael Jackson)* (2005), from which Jackson himself is absent, yet conjured in the bodies of several on-screen German fans singing their way through *Thriller*. They are each singing the same songs, yet every song is made different, multiple, by the person singing it: that quiet one there who is hardly moving, the flirty belly-dancing one, the cocksure lookalike one, the middle-aged geeky one. They are all passionate, knowingly on show, but imbued with self-possession, the music a common language. A parting evocation of what the artists themselves saw and found in Michael Jackson.

The New York Review of Books Daily, 2018

Edward Enninful: Fashioning Change

August 2020 saw no soca floats sliding along Ladbroke Grove with masqueraders at their tails. No pink feathered wings or soft turquoise shimmies, no sequinned bodysuits or giant skyward plumes of headwear. Carnival was off, like all mass gatherings in late Covid lockdown, London creeping tentatively from its inner rooms, the streets still spare, the air still choked with grief. No curry goat or jerk-pan smoke rose up into the city trees, quenching hungry dancing crowds between swigs of rum punch. And the music, the great churning music of the Caribbean islands, of Black Britain, of Africa and the Americas, did not thump to the foundations of the Portobello terraces, making them tremble.

All of this would have been part of a normal summer to Edward Enninful while growing up in the area in the 1980s. His mother, Grace, might look out of the window of her sewing room in their house on Kensal Road, right on the Notting Hill Carnival route, and see some manifestation of Trinidad going by, or a reggae crew, wrapped in amazing sculptures of bikini and shiny see-through hosiery. Edward, one among a ready-made posse of six siblings, would stay out late and take it in, all that sound and spectacle, which for decades has been the triumphant annual pinnacle of London's cultural and racial multiplicity.

It was this world that nurtured his creativity and helped shape the vision he has brought to the pages of British *Vogue* since being appointed editor-in-chief in 2017. 'I was always othered – you know, gay, working class, black,' Enninful says on a nostalgic walk through the streets of Ladbroke Grove, where he moved with his family from Ghana at the age of thirteen. 'So for me it was very important with *Vogue* to normalise the marginalised, because if you don't see it, you don't think it's normal.' Today Enninful is one of the most powerful leaders in his industry, sitting at the intersection of fashion and media, two fields that are undergoing long-overdue change and scrambling to make up for years of negligence and malpractice. Since becoming the only black editor in history to head any of the supremely influential twenty-six *Vogue* magazines, he has been tipped as the successor to Anna Wintour, the iconic editor of American *Vogue* and artistic director of Condé Nast. The company is navigating, on top of an advertising market battered by the Covid-19 pandemic, public controversies around representation both in its offices and on its pages, and Enninful's UK vision therefore comes at a critical moment.

'I wanted to reflect what I saw here growing up,' he tells me, 'to show the world as this incredibly rich, cultured place. I wanted every woman to be able to find themselves in the magazine.' He chose the British model Adwoa Aboah to front his first issue: 'When others took steps, Edward took massive strides, showing the importance of our visibility and stories,' she says. Covers since have featured the likes of Oprah Winfrey, Rihanna, Judi Dench (at eighty-five, British *Vogue*'s oldest cover star), Madonna and footballer Marcus Rashford, photographed for this year's September issue by Misan Harriman, the first black male photographer to shoot a British *Vogue* cover in its 104-year history. Under Enninful's leadership the magazine has morphed from an elitist, white-run glossy of the bourgeois oblivious into a diverse and inclusive on-point fashion platform, shaking up the imagery, tracking the contemporary pain, in his own words, 'following the conversation'. Its shelf presence is different – more substance, more political – and perhaps in part because of it, the shelf as a whole looks different. No more do black women search mainstream newsstands in vain for visions of themselves. Now we are ubiquitous in my newsagent, in my corner shop, and it really wasn't that hard; all it took was to give a black man some power, to give someone with a gift, a voice and a view from the margin a seat at the table.

'My blackness has never been a hindrance to me,' Enninful says. Yet he is no stranger to the passing abuses of systematic racism. On a Wednesday in mid-July, while entering British *Vogue*'s London headquarters, he was racially profiled by a security guard who told him to enter via the loading bay instead. 'Just because our timelines and weekends are returning to normal, we cannot let the world return to how it was,' he wrote on Twitter. This summer, in the wake of the worldwide Black Lives Matter protests sparked by the killing of George Floyd, we are seeing a seismic reckoning across industries, scrutinising who is doing what and who is not doing enough to bring about real change in equality and representation. 'My problem is that there's a lot of virtue signalling going on,' he says. 'But everyone's listening now, and we need to take advantage of that. This is not the time for tiptoeing.'

We meet at Ladbroke Grove Tube station in a late-summer noon bereft of its carnival and permanently scarred by Grenfell. When anticipating an interview with the leader of a historic luxury fashion bible, it's tempting to have inferior thoughts about your Nissan or your Clarks boot collection or your latest unlatest something, but Enninful, now forty-eight, is unassuming, arriving in a loose navy suit, pale-blue shirt and shades, the only giveaway to his sartorial imperium the no socks with his brogues. He is warm and wearily flamboyant, bearing the close-shouldered tilt of the lifelong hard worker (he rises at 5 a.m. most days to meditate before work).

These days he resides towards Lancaster Gate, on the posher

side of Ladbroke Grove, with his long-term partner the film-maker Alec Maxwell and their Boston Terrier Ru Enninful, who has his own Instagram account and whose daily walking was a saving grace during lockdown. But the London Underground is where Enninful's journey into fashion began, one day on the train in a pair of ripped blue jeans, when he was spotted by stylist Simon Foxton as a potential model for *i-D*, the avant-garde fashion magazine. Being only sixteen, a shy, sheltered kid who grew up in a Ghanaian army barracks and had moved to the UK less than four years before, of course he had to ask his mother, who was sceptical. Albeit a clothes fanatic herself, a professional seamstress and regular riffler (with Edward) through the markets of Portobello and Brixton for fabrics, Grace was wary of the hedonistic London style vortex, the enormity of the new land, and reluctant to release her son into its mouth. He begged. He wore her down. 'I knew I couldn't just walk away from this, that something special was going to come out of it.'

He never had the knack for modelling, he says with character-istic humility. 'I was terrible at it. I hated the castings, all that objectifying. But I loved the process and the craft of creating an image. I used it as a study, to progress to something else.' He soon moved to the other side of the lens, assisting on shoots and assembling image concepts and narratives, a particular approach to styling that impressed *i-D* enough to hire him as their young-est ever fashion director at only eighteen, a post he held for the next twenty years. Without the courtesy designer clothes that were later routinely at his fingertips, he would customise, shred, dye and bargain for the right look, using the skills he'd developed at home in the sewing room. 'I realised that I could say a lot with fashion,' he says, 'that it wasn't just about clothes, but could tell a story of the times we're in, about people's experiences in life. And that freedom to portray the world as you saw it.'

What was innate to Enninful – this blend of skilled creativity with the perception of difference as normal, as both subject and audience – was relatively unique in an industry dominated by white, colonial notions of beauty and mainstream. Legendary Somali supermodel Iman remembers a 2014 *W* magazine shoot in which she, Naomi Campbell and Rihanna were cast by Enninful, the publication's then style director, wearing Balmain, designed by Olivier Rousteing. 'It's sad to say but until Edward appeared, no one at the mainstream fashion magazines would have cared to commission a portrait exclusively featuring three women of colour, and furthermore who were all wearing clothes designed by a person of colour,' she says. 'He's an editor in vocation and a reformer at heart, compelled to spur woefully needed social change.'

He shows me his various old haunts and abodes, the top-floor bedsit where he used to haul bags of styling gear up the stairs, the Lisboa and O'Porto cafés of Golborne Road – or 'Little Morocco' – where he'd sit for hours chewing the fat with people like make-up artist Pat McGrath, Kate Moss, Nick Kamen and photographer David Sims. He met Moss when she was fourteen, at his first modelling gig (an ad for Pepe Jeans), along with an eighteen-year-old Steve McQueen who had also been spotted by Foxton. Namedrops fall from his lips like insignificant diamonds – stylists, photographers, celebrities – but he navigates his domain in a manner apparently uncommon among fashion's gatekeepers. Winfrey says of him, 'I have never experienced in all my dealings with people in that world anyone who was more kind and generous of spirit. I mean, it just doesn't happen.'

Her photoshoot for the August 2018 cover of British *Vogue* left Winfrey feeling 'empress-like', and she ascribes his understanding of black female beauty to having been raised by a black mother. 'Edward understands that images are political, that they say who and what matters,' she adds. Enninful's father Crosby, a major in the Ghanaian army who was part of UN operations in Egypt and Lebanon, had thought that his bright, studious son would eventually grow out of his fascination with clothes and become a lawyer. But three months into an English literature degree at Goldsmiths, studying Hardy, Austen and the classics, thinking maybe he'd be a writer, or indeed a lawyer, Edward quit to take up the position at *i-D*. His father did not speak to him for around fifteen years, into the next century, until Grace suffered a stroke and entered a long illness. 'Now that I'm older I realise he just wanted to protect us. He's come to understand that I had to follow my heart and forge my own path.'

He credits his parents for his strong work ethic – 'drummed into you from a very early age by black parents, that you have to work twice as hard' – and his Ghanaian heritage for his eye for colour. His approach to fashion as narrative comes from the 'childish games I would play with my mother', creating characters around the clothes, sketching them out. 'I can't just shoot clothes off the runway,' he says. 'There always has to be a character, and that character has to have an inner life.' Since Grace's death three years ago, his father has lived alone by the Grand Union Canal and is very proud of his son, particularly of the OBE awarded to him in 2016 for his services to diversity in the fashion industry, which he accepted for the sake of his parents 'who had come here with nothing'. Queen Elizabeth II, incidentally, is high on Enninful's list of *Vogue* cover dreams.

The British *Vogue* passed on to her successor by former editor-in-chief Alexandra Shulman was starkly different from today's rendition. During her twenty-five years in charge, only twelve covers out of 306 featured black women, and she left behind an almost entirely white workforce. Now the editorial team is 25 per cent people of colour – 'I needed certain lieutenants in place,' Enninful says – and similar shufflings are being called for

over at Condé Nast in New York. He is reluctant, though, to
tarnish names any further, maintaining that Shulman 'repre-
sented her time, I represent mine' and declining to comment on
circumstances at the US headquarters.

Enninful's rise is particularly meaningful to people like André
Leon Talley, former editor at large of American *Vogue*, where
Enninful also worked as a contributing editor. Talley describes
the new British *Vogue* as 'extraordinary', and was joyous at the
appointment, which he considers one of Condé Nast's greatest
moments. 'He speaks for the unsung heroes, particularly those
outside the privileged white world that *Vogue* originally stood
for. He has changed what a fashion magazine should be.'

'I'm a custodian,' Enninful says of his role, sitting in a sumptuous alcove of the club bar at Electric House. '*Vogue* existed before
I came, and it will still exist when I leave, but I knew that I had to
go in there and do what I really believed in. It's our responsibility
as storytellers or image makers to try to disrupt the status quo.'
Ironically, though, he does not see himself as an activist, rather as
someone who is unafraid to tackle political issues and educate
others, while remaining firmly within the *Vogue* lens. 'They said
black girls on the cover don't sell,' he says. 'People thought diversity equals downmarket, but we've shown that it's just good for
business.' British *Vogue*'s digital traffic is up 51 per cent since he
took over. He previously edited the 2008 Black Issue of *Vogue*
Italia, which featured only black models and black women and
sold out in the US and the UK in just seventy-two hours.

Since the incident with the security guard in July – which
Enninful reveals was not isolated and had happened before (the
culprit, a third-party employee, was dismissed from headquarters) – building staff have been added to the company's
diversity-and-inclusion trainings, covering micro-aggressions,
unconscious bias and mentoring. Enninful would also like to see
bursaries put in place for middle-management, 'because we

forget sometimes that the culture of a place does not allow you to go from being a student to the top'. In 2013 he tweeted about another incident, where he was seated in the second row at a Paris couture show while his white counterparts were seated in front. 'I get racially profiled all the time,' he says, going right back to his first experience of being stopped and searched by police in Bayswater as a teenager, which 'petrified' him. 'When I was younger I would've been hurt and withdrawn, but now I will let you know that this is not OK. People tend to think that if you're successful it eliminates you, but it can happen any day. The difference now is that I have the platform to speak about it and point it out. You have to use whatever platform you have to make sure there's change in the world. The only way we can smash systematic racism is by doing it together.'

Activism, then, is intrinsic. Fashion is altruism, as much as story and craft, as much as the will to capture beauty. For Enninful there is no limitation to the radicalism that is possible through his line of work. Rather than the seemingly unattainable elements of style (the £350 zirconia ring, the £2,275 coat) obscuring the moral fibre of the message, the invitation to think and see more openly, instead the style leads you to it, perhaps even inviting you to assemble something similar within the boundaries of your real, more brutal, less elevated existence. 'Relatable luxury,' he calls it, and though it's difficult to imagine exactly how one might evoke a £2,275 coat without his customising skills and magical thinking, I am inclined to accept the notion, partly because I saw soul singer Celeste in a £1,450 dress in the September issue and think I might give it a try. Anything is possible. 'I still feel like I'm at the beginning,' he says with palpable optimism. 'I feel the fire of something new.'

Thandiwe Newton: That's My Name

The story begins with the thundering mist of Victoria Falls, 1972. A Zimbabwean princess and a lab technician from Cornwall were driving along a bumpy road about to enjoy a sardine snack. When the sardine can was opened, the oil spilled all over the woman's dress and she laughed her head off. The man thought, 'I need to be with this woman,' and there were rainbows criss-crossing the sky from the magic of the mist and the sun above the crashing water. On that trip, contained in this magic, a child was conceived. They named her Thandiwe, meaning 'beloved' in Zulu. She grew up to be one of the most successful Black-British actresses of her time.

Switch now to Cornwall, three years later. 'I mean holy hell,' she says. 'We may as well have been the first black people anyone had ever seen. We didn't have *conditioner*. We didn't have *anything*.' There, her mother, the granddaughter of a Shona chief, hence her royal lineage, became an NHS health worker and her father took over his family's antiques business. Meanwhile Thandiwe and her younger brother attended a Catholic primary school run by joyless nuns, where she was once excluded from a class photograph for sporting cornrows and generally made to feel like an in-house missionary project, and where the W of her name drifted inwards, out of sight and earshot, in a futile hope to make her feel less different. She eventually replaced the greens and shores of the West Country with the urban smoke of north-west London, similar to the way her father, also eager for escape, had randomly chosen Zambia on the map of Africa in search of

the roots of the blues because of how much he loved Chuck
Berry; 'that's how cool my dad is.'

I first interviewed Thandiwe Newton around twenty years
ago in the lobby of a Covent Garden hotel for the cover of
Pride magazine (this cover story is about that much time over-
due). She was wearing gym clothes and looked wistfully
childlike. Nowadays you would not see her in a gym, you will
not see her jogging ('I *hate* exercise'), but back then she was
preparing to star opposite Tom Cruise in *Mission: Impossible II*
and was required to perform stunts. She played the beautiful
thief and love interest Nyah Nordoff-Hall; a couple of years
before that she had played the title role in the Toni Morrison
adaptation *Beloved*; a year before that the waifish, moody
singer in *Gridlock'd* alongside Tupac Shakur, who she described
to me as 'the sweetest person' and 'so funny'. She later won a
BAFTA for her performance in *Crash* and became the first
black woman to play a prominent character in a *Star Wars*
film.

Despite these achievements, she has never quite received the
glory she deserves as a British national treasure and screen icon:
that coy and elfin face, the dignified grace and the remarkable
versatility of her talent, this is a career both longstanding and
undervalued. Her roles have been varied and cross-genre –
among her favourites is Olanna in 2013's *Half of a Yellow
Sun* – spanning three decades and gradually becoming aligned
with her political activism, culminating in her Emmy-winning
and Golden Globe-nominated performance as the android
brothel-madam Maeve Millay in the HBO hit sci-fi series *Westworld*, this year shooting its fourth season. 'I can tell when
people haven't watched *Westworld* because they just think
I'm being naked and sexy in it,' Newton says. 'But I love how
subversive it is. Wherever I position myself now, I don't want to
be part of the problem, I want to be part of the solution. I'm not

for hire anymore. I'm not going to speak your story or say your words if I don't feel they could've come from me.'

This time we meet in the flattening sphere of Zoom on the day that Trump defiled the Capitol. The streets of northwest London are spare. Britain is in its third national lockdown. Approaching the screen from across her warmly lit bedroom, she arrives as a light, bright presence, wearing hoop earrings and an orange sweatshirt, looking, at forty-eight, basically unaged. 'I've changed a whole lot,' she laughs knowingly. 'Many lives have been lived since then.' We spend some time reflecting back, she's read some of my fiction and is loving and complimentary towards it, even thanks me for it, and tells me she was thrilled when *Vogue* paired us for this story. We talk for three hours and a further two the following week because there's more to say. She is a passionate and expansive conversationalist, leaping from one subject to another (factory farms, colonialism, mother-hood, literature), easily moved to tears and somehow tactile, even in this format. She is a vegan on political and humanitarian grounds and counts among her heroes the Congolese gynae-cologist, human-rights activist and Nobel Peace laureate Denis Mukwege.

In other parts of the house are her children – Booker, seven, Nico, sixteen, and Ripley, twenty, whose girlfriend is staying with them during lockdown – and her husband of twenty-three years, the screenwriter and director Ol Parker, who pops into the room occasionally to bring her a drink or remind her about a meeting – she's in discussions about adapting the story of a black-versus-white shoot-out in 1940s Cornwall between American soldiers, and is due back on set for the forth-coming CIA thriller *All the Old Knives*. This year also sees the release of sci-fi romance *Reminiscence*, the directorial debut of *Westworld* co-creator Lisa Joy, in which she stars with Hugh Jackman, and the completion of the timely neo-Western *God's*

Country. When offered the *Westworld* role in 2014, Newton was close to retiring from acting. She had just had her last baby, quit her role in the Canadian police drama *Rogue* because of mistreatment and was turning her attention to writing. Now, with Hollywood knocking more loudly than ever, it seems likely that we will see her ascend to the echelons of middle-age thespian darlinghood, like a Helen Mirren or Regina King, starlit in maturity.

While amazed at her resurgence she is mindful of its shadow. 'I find that acting takes more and more away from me,' she says with candour, 'because I'm more connected to myself than I've ever been, whereas before I was delighted to get an excuse to go off to another personality. I couldn't wait to get away from myself, truly, I had such low self-esteem. Acting was where I felt whole.' The nuns hadn't helped. Nor had the dance teacher at her extracurricular lessons in Cornwall who'd annually bypassed the brilliant brown ballerina at trophy time. Newton pursued her dance aspirations at a performing arts secondary boarding school in Hertfordshire before moving to London but was curtailed by a back injury and switched her focus to acting. It was disconcerting, too, that this same brownness was to become a site of manipulation, confusion and psychological violence upon entering the movie industry. The summer she took her GCSEs, when auditioning for her debut role alongside Nicole Kidman in *Flirting*, the Australian director John Duigan was not quite satisfied with her shade. 'Can you be a bit darker?' he said. 'I dunno,' said Thandiwe. 'Be darker by Monday,' he said. So she spent the weekend covered in coconut oil and frantically bronzing. 'Got the role. Colourism has just been the funniest. I've been too black, not black enough. I'm always *black*. I'm just like, whadda people want!' It was Duigan, incidentally, who went on to play the real-life role of a sexual predator to that darkened, virginal sixteen-year-old schoolgirl once filming began in Australia. That definitely didn't help.

Newton has been a staunch and persistent whistle-blower on the subject of sexual violence and harassment, in Hollywood and beyond, for decades. Long before #MeToo and Time's Up, she was challenging the great wall of silence and enablement surrounding the high crimes and misdemeanours of the entertainment moguls, the Weinsteins and Epsteins, the Cosbys and Kellys, while meeting angry rebuff and gaslighting along the way, at one point terminating a contract with a publicist who begged her to stop talking about being sexually abused because it was 'not good for your reputation'. But for her, silence was not an option. Speaking out was a reflex, an imperative, a reach for what had been lost and some justice to cushion the void. 'There's a moment where the ghost of me changed, you know,' she says thoughtfully, zoning back in time, eyes hardened, 'and it was then, it was sixteen. He derailed me from myself utterly. I was traumatised. It was a kind of PTSD for sure. I was so distraught and appalled that a director had abused a young actress, and that it was happening elsewhere, minors getting abused and how *fucked up* it was. I was basically waiting for someone to come along and say, "Well, what shall we *do* about this?"'

And they did, in droves, the women. 'Me Too', the phrase coined by activist Tarana Burke in 2006, became a hashtag storm that would morph into one of the largest social uprisings in modern history, defying structures of inequity and leading to such incredible things as a woman and a man earning exactly the same amount of money for exactly the same amount of work on set, as recently occurred at HBO among the *Westworld* cast – Newton and Evan Rachel Wood now earn the same as their male counterparts, setting a precedent in the industry that Newton wants to see normalised. 'It wasn't a celebration. I was disgusted,' she says, and she is pragmatic about the continuing need to challenge silencing and abuses of power. 'Even though people know they can speak out now, there is still the fear of losing their job. I mean literally, people still say, "There's someone else who could take this position if you're not happy", that kind of shit. I do think studio heads need to take much more responsibility.' Newton sees the money she earns from her acting as 'compensation' for the emotional turmoil caused by such abuses of power – the casting director who filmed and shared intimate audition footage of her at eighteen, that prior derailment at sixteen and its lethal fusion with an ego stunted by early racism. 'I didn't have a harbour to go back to. I didn't have a place, a lighthouse. I was just lost all the time. I punished my body to try and find my heart.'

The violations by Duigan lasted five years, two of which were termed a 'relationship' after he sought Newton's parents' blessing for her to be his girlfriend when she was eighteen, while asking her to hide their previous intimacy. If passers-by questioned with their eyes what this much older man was doing with this young girl, he would tell her that they were being racist, towards her, and she believed him. 'It was textbook, really boring textbook.' At twenty, Newton managed to free herself and moved into her first flat, there continuing with her anthropology degree at Cambridge and doing two more films with Duigan out of shame and guilt for 'abandoning' him. As a coping mechanism for these warped feelings, the ability to control her body's intake of food became her friend, and thus ensued 'the most horrific dance with something that's supposed to bring you life', which would almost kill her. One night, just before the filming of *Gridlock'd* in 1996, she was rescued: 'I was lying in bed, so thin, and my heart was beating against my ribcage so hard that I could see it, and my friend Jessica called. I said "Jessica, I'm worried I'm going to die." And that was it. I suddenly realised there was something very, very dangerous and dark within. She said, "You've got to go and talk to somebody." '

Therapy and personal development have benefited Newton substantially over time, in particular the Hoffman Process, as well as the philosophy of Buddhism. Years later, that dance with death no longer rears its head. When asked what advice she would give to someone struggling with an eating disorder, she takes great care in answering. 'I wish I could talk to you,' she says, 'and the questions that I would ask you would range all over your life, from the first memory, because you're unique, and the same power that is driving you to hurt yourself, you can change that to a power to nurture yourself, once you find the kernel of truth that has been denied you.'

Married to Parker at twenty-five, Newton progressed her career impressively through her twenties and thirties while she became a mother, always taking her family with her on projects abroad. But roles were lost in her refusal to play to racial and sexual stereotyping, such as 2000's *Charlie's Angels*, when derogatory and ignorant comments made by former Sony Pictures head Amy Pascal about what a black female character should be – sexy, not university educated (Pascal says she has no memory of the event) – made Newton quit, and she was replaced by Lucy Liu. On the release of *Beloved*, Newton was asked by a Hollywood Foreign Press Association journalist, 'Will you sign my magazine in African?', and this made her rebuff the organisation for years. Most of all she refused to pander to silencing. 'I have a seventh sense for abuse and abusers,' she says, 'which I believe is one of the reasons why I was rejected a lot in Hollywood. I'll talk about it until the cows come home, because I know I'll be helping someone.'

It was the American playwright, performer and feminist Eve Ensler who enabled Newton to move out of the victim mindset instilled in her by trauma. In 2011 she went to see Ensler perform

The Vagina Monologues at the King's Head Theatre in Islington, on a casual invitation along the lines of 'Do you wanna come and see that crazy lady talking about fannies?' Afterwards the two women got talking and a whole other way of thinking emerged: 'It was the first time, apart from with my husband, where I didn't feel ashamed about what had happened. She was just this amazing, radiant energy; it was infectious.' Following this meeting Newton became part of a community of victim-turned-survivors trying to make a change, a kind of sisterhood, where self-hurt or self-hate was replaced with a common transformative purpose. 'When I started joining in I found myself around a lot more people of colour. Isn't that strange?' she says. 'Well, because there are so many women of colour who've been abused, and who are the spine of their community or the spine of their family. Black women are truly the nexus where all of this overlaps. Think of what else has the potential to heal if we support and care for black women.'

Newton has an activist soul, turned outwards to the world, magnanimous and wise, sharpened into an instrument of power. Alongside her film and TV commitments she advocates for the African American Policy Forum and the #sayhername campaign founded by her friend Kimberlé Crenshaw, who coined the term 'intersectionality'. She is also a board member of Eve Ensler's V-Day, through which she has supported women survivors of sexual violence in Congo with the City of Joy project, and helped establish One Billion Rising, which campaigns to end violence against women, spurred by the UN statistic that one in three women will be abused in her lifetime. Activism now far outweighs acting in order of importance – it meant a lot to Newton that the OBE she was awarded in 2018 was for services to charity as well as to film. 'Individuals count,' she says, buoyed by the hope and possibility of our troubled time. 'We can make a difference.'

In Shona custom, the royal lineage passes down through generations, which means that Newton's two daughters, Ripley and Nico, are also princesses, like their grandmother and great-grandmother, as well as Thandiwe herself. Her Twitter bio reads simply 'Mother', and this seems the most central of all of her roles. 'When I had my children, it was like, *Oh, finally I can love me*. I could love them and not in any way question my love, whether it was worthy of them. As soon as I had my baby I became *everything* I ever wanted to be, because that's what she deserved.' Her youngest daughter Nico, at sixteen, is already four years into her own acting career, with lead parts in *Dumbo* and *The Third Day*. And there is not a chance in high hell that this mother is going to let the same story unfold. She says fiercely, with a fire in her eyes, 'I went to every photoshoot with her. If there was an issue with the photographer, if there was inappropriate language, I was on it, didn't give a fuck what anyone thought. When it was time for her to get an agent, I spent a month auditioning for one, even though I knew half of them.' She has also worked hard to implant in her children emotional intelligence, awareness and a high moral sense: one of her proudest moments was when Ripley called Boris Johnson a cunt to his face at a Harry Potter theatre trip.

Newton's parents live in London now and their own proudest moment is their daughter's OBE – her mother never misses an opportunity to watch the royals on TV ('She's got more national pride than I have'). Newton, though, posits herself as a Londoner as opposed to British, and remembers a British newspaper pointing out when she won the BAFTA that she was not really British because one of her parents was black. 'I remember thinking, But it's a British win! Why don't you wanna take that? Why would you not wanna dig that and embrace it and feel really good?' She is pained by the same old period dramas and lack of diversity that have traditionally sent British actors of colour seeking opportunity and visibility across the Atlantic. But things are changing, and she is one of the engines of change, a role model for little brown girls who want to be dancers or Hollywood actors or activists or one day see themselves on the cover of *Vogue*. It was essential to her that the clothes used in this long-belated photoshoot reflect her dual heritage, thus a bold Versace suit paired with a length of African fabric bought from Shepherd's Bush, and the work of designers such as Duro Olowu, Kenneth Ize and Cheyenne Kimora featuring alongside European-heritage brands.

No longer is Newton afraid of the red carpet because of how much it reminded her of her invisibility, and she looks forward to a future where the illusion of race will no longer narrow who we are. 'The thing I'm most grateful for in our business right now is being in the company of others who truly see me. And to not be complicit in the objectification of black people as "others", which is what happens when you're the only one.' All her future films will be credited with Thandiwe Newton, after the W in 'Thandiwe' was carelessly missed out from her first credit. Now she's in control. Many lives lived and she's come out triumphant, preserved in the magic of the mist and sun that made her, and wanted her to shine. 'That's my name. It's always been my name. I'm taking back what's mine.'

British *Vogue*, 2021

Lynette Yiadom-Boakye:
Fly in League with the Night

This sentence glitters on a wall at the entrance to British-Ghanaian artist Lynette Yiadom-Boakye's solo show at Tate Britain: 'But the idea of infinity, of a life and a world of infinite possibilities, where anything is possible for you, unconstrained by the nightmare fantasies of others, to have the presence of mind to walk as wildly as you will, that's what I think about most, that is the direction I've always wanted to move in.'[2] The artist's own words, which bear an extra shine given the literary branch of her work (poems, occasional prose, animal fables), and which, in their aspiration towards an existential liberty, convey the achieved atmosphere of her paintings, their auras of cryptic distance, yet bold, living presence, as if the act of creating them were the wish itself.

The myriad figures in these paintings walk wildly, in their loose dark lines and muted landscapes, their casual gestures and gentle staring. Their thoughts are entirely their own, as they look off into a dappled sepia with a touch of gold in it, such as the woman caught in contemplation in *Penny For Them* (2014), or sit troubled and fatigued in the *Pale For The Rapture* (2016) diptych with its contrasting stripe-check sofas. They hold council with birds, an owl perched in hand or a shockingly bright parrot glowing from the grip of a man's enveloping gloom. Sometimes they are dancing, like the young men at the ballet barre in *A Concentration* (2018), or laughing, inwardly smiling, or looking straight at one another as are the two boys in *No Need of Speech* (2018). This painting in particular evokes an emotional charge, given the routine reduction of black boys in mainstream imagery, but Yiadom-Boakye wants to capture the subject beyond all that, in the freer, almost possible, infinite space. Her men, women and children, conjured mostly from her imagination, have an air of something heavy having been thrown off. They are unconstrained by those 'nightmare fantasies' and allowed simply to live, to be; strident yet languid, close to joy. 'I don't like to paint victims,' the artist has said.

Fly in League with the Night is the first major survey of Yiadom-Boakye's work, featuring some eighty oil paintings spanning nearly two decades, from her training at the Royal Academy Schools to recent pieces created in her east London studio and, in smaller scale, at her south London home. The paintings, some on canvas, some on herringbone linen, are hung low for impact and without adherence to chronology; instead, they are arranged in communication with one another so that each room has a singular atmosphere. There are the sharp, spectacular reds of the opening room where a brash, carnal early work, *First* (2003), is positioned next to the refined yet no less imposing subject of *Any Number Of Preoccupations* (2010) in his draping vermillion gown and white slippers (a direct nod to John Singer Sargent's *Dr Pozzi at Home*); while adjacent lies a crimson-tongued fox beneath a stool on which a man sits, carefree and leaning forward, both welcoming and enclosed in darkness. Further on in the show, a gathering of paler, shadowy outdoor scenes featuring figures walking and talking, lounging on sand or silently looking out, give a calmer, more luminous effect – a highlight here is *Condor And The Mole* (2011), one of Yiadom-Boakye's comparatively rare depictions of children, two black girls playing on a rocky beach against a grey horizon, the kind of rural image we have scarcely seen before in this style of painting.

It is the absence of black subjects in traditional Western portraiture, from which Yiadom-Boakye draws much of her influence, that makes these paintings intrinsically revolutionary, constituting on one level a virtual reinvention of the form itself. But it is this artist's approach to paint, her relationship to it, the way she makes it speak, that is most compelling. Her many darknesses are rich and hued, never hollow, faintly misted by a suggestion of green, within the green the yellow, the brown, or there is the dim stretch of night purple behind the bright hat feather of *Six Birds In The Bush* (2015), making the soft brown of the face and the beige of the eyes almost move towards you. With a flash of white she makes a laughter come, or smoke drift. White dances monochrome circles on a T-shirt against the dark of *11pm Tuesday* (2010), making fabric fly and lift around the slightly radiating figure, thereby making breeze, light, air. The colours don't end; these are journeys, adventures in colour. They play and signal and decide for themselves, the artist acting as a conduit: those pink and mustard ties in what I think of as the avuncular paintings, tenderly rendered depictions of ageing men chinking and linking arms, and then the jubilant, never-ending greens of the four young men in *Complication* (2013), which was a personal favourite for its quiet humour and brotherly love.

The titles of Yiadom-Boakye's portraits are 'an extra brush-mark', she calls them, and can be thought of as bridges of mystery between her painting and her writing. There are no distracting or pre-emptive explanatory captions accompanying the images, only the possible stories that might be conjured by their names, depending on who is looking at them. Likewise, the paintings are devoid of any temporal specificities of attire, object or defined locales, and the subjects themselves are imagined beings rather than real, arrivals of character through a process of live composition, begun without preliminary sketching or outline. These arrivals are made possible by the clearing of space, the stripping back of reality so that the human figure might be captured in its immediate lucidity, unmarred by the dampening associations of societal identification and circumstance. Toni Morrison once wrote of the work of James Baldwin, 'You gave us ourselves to think about',[3] and Baldwin being held dear by Yiadom-Boakye, this seems a fitting observation. In her thoughtful, unhampered and magnificent images of black figures, she gives us ourselves to think about by drawing what has been held in shadow – misunderstood, ignored, unwitnessed – into the light of near transcendence. And she does not deny the shadow, but makes it part of the story, a site of permanent yet quietened resistance.

Yiadom-Boakye's work is a triumphant demonstration of the power of the artist to recreate, reclaim and restore the world for the time of looking. I found it difficult to leave behind the kindness of this show, but the voice of the paint went with me, and those words in particular, written on the wall above our heads, 'a life and a world of infinite possibilities'.

Apollo, 2021

Viola Davis: Woman King

Many of us had existential thoughts during lockdown, and assuaged them with new hobbies, time-consuming pursuits. We did thousand-piece puzzles. We crocheted and knitted. We learned new songs on our guitars, baked overzealously and connected with our plantlife. For Viola Davis, knocking around in her five-million-dollar mansion in Toluca Lake, Los Angeles, it was writing, though the nature of it was less assuagement than staring into the coalface of an existential crisis. Who am I? What is my life supposed to mean? If this isn't it – the Oscar-winning, the formidable trail of accolades, the palatial bathrooms and saltwater pool – then what is?

'I lost my mind during the pandemic,' she tells me from her bedroom, dressed pre-photoshoot in a grey sweatshirt and loose woollen hat. 'I just wandered around this house like Mary Tyrone in *Long Day's Journey Into Night*.' She laughs about it (she has a deep laugh and a deep, mighty voice inherited from her grandmother Mozell Logan), but the memoir resulting from the time spent writing is anything but light. She has a story to tell, a gripping, emotive, at times spine-tingling story, with pathos and pain, triumph and redemption, setting a new bench-mark of substance for the celebrity confessional. *Finding Me* is a page-turner, written with narrative know-how and stylistic competence. Over a matter of months – interrupted by the filming of *The First Lady*, in which she plays Michelle Obama, and *The Woman King*, a historical drama set in the Kingdom of Dahomey, both projects from her company JuVee Productions – she grappled on the page with the spectre of her poverty-stricken childhood and her subsequent thorny rise to the top, a place that turned out to be less comfortable than imagined.

'Whenever you're still, whenever you're quiet, whenever you put everything down, then everything in your life comes into full focus. It comes at you like a jackhammer,' she says of the big Covid pause. But it was not only the pandemic that led her to the blank screen. The crisis was already in process. 'I think it's been happening really ever since my status started to rise. When it first rises it's nothing but excitement, nothing but an understanding that this is a culmination of your hard work, your talent. You just feel like God has blessed you – I still feel that. And then it moves along: what no one tells you about being "on top" is the minutiae of it, the cost of it, the pressure of it, the responsibility, and finally the disillusionment. You feel like you've found something you love to do and you've made it, your life's all sewn up – but then you hit it, and it's just a level of emptiness, of wondering what your life means, and then you crash and burn. I had to go back to the source and revisit my life, revisit my stories, to sort of catapult me into something so I could find home – find me. I'd been lost in it all.'

In 2016, with her Academy Award win for best supporting actress for her role in *Fences*, based on the August Wilson play, Viola Davis became the first African American to achieve the triple crown of an Oscar, Tony and Emmy for acting (the Tony was for a Broadway role in Wilson's *King Hedley II*, the Emmy for the TV legal thriller *How To Get Away With Murder*). She is the most nominated black woman in the history of the Academy Awards (she received nominations for *Ma Rainey's Black Bottom*, another Wilson adaptation, as well as *The Help* and *Doubt*) and has been ranked in the top ten in the *New York Times*'s list of the greatest actors of the twenty-first century. Her execution of her roles is both exacting and magnanimous, ever astute, possessing a haunting integrity that makes each character she plays seem profoundly known, tangible and self-possessed. The consummate humble artist, she deems the resulting fame and glory secondary to the work, is modest with her trophies, dismissive of efforts by her actor husband of almost nineteen years, Julius Tennon, and their adopted daughter, Genesis, to splash them around the house. 'If it were up to me all the awards would be in the garage,' she says. 'I mean, it's just not my style. It's a bit too much. Listen, it's not that I haven't looked at the Oscar or whatever and thought, wow, that's pretty awesome. I'm very grateful, but, you know, you can't live there. Soon as you get it, you walk off the stage, you're an Oscar winner, but then it's like, and now what? And then you gotta go on to the next job and start all over again with that imposter syndrome.'

The memoir begins with a spunky eight-year-old Viola, a 'sassy mess' with torn socks and too-big shoes who every day is chased home from school by a group of racist boys throwing rocks, bricks, tree branches and pine cones. In order to help her defend herself, her mother, Mae Alice Davis, who worked as a maid and factory worker and was active in the civil-rights movement, gives her a shiny blue crochet needle to stab them with and tells her to walk, not run. They are the only African American family in the densely populated, drug-stained town of Central Falls, Rhode Island, having relocated there from South Carolina. They live in a condemned, rat-infested building, often with no hot water, gas or electricity, and the rats are so bad and bold that they eat the faces of Viola's dolls and jump onto her bed at night searching for food. She never goes into the kitchen because of them. She wets the bed until she is fourteen and, limited to soapless cold water wipe-downs, she and her four sisters regularly attend school reeking. Plus, there are fires – they become 'experienced fire-escape climbers'. There is one occasion when Viola's mother performs a superhuman leap to rescue her when she is too afraid to jump, yet this firetrap remains their home for another two years. 'No one cares about the conditions in which the unwanted live,' Davis writes. 'You're invisible, a blame factor that allows the more advantaged to be let off the hook from your misery.'

Part of the legacy of that time is that Davis refuses to grant her daughter's wish for a pet rat. Again she laughs with her close, characteristic humour and affability, while at the same time is gravely serious about the impact on her identity of being raised, not just poor, but 'po', an extremity beyond. 'I have an understanding of poverty that probably a lot of people don't, so I don't romanticise it,' she says. 'I know what deprivation feels like, and the most important thing that it gave me is compassion. There is something about knowing the road, and having it hard, and being baptised by fire, that you begin to have a true awareness of what it means for people who live in poverty, and how difficult or impossible it is to get out. It's made me see the other side of life, as opposed to just sitting at a cocktail party talking about poverty the same way, I mean, I don't know, the same way you would talk about a Picasso painting. I have a front-row seat.'

In addition to the 'dumpster-diving', food stamps and persistent hunger, there was her father's alcoholism and violence to contend with, rendering the family home a 'war zone'. Dan Davis was a racetrack horse groomer as well as being 'pretty good' on the guitar and harmonica. Davis writes fondly of going to the stables with him, of his fierce protection of his family and his enthusiasm around festive periods; he was big on Valentine's Day and every year put up a Christmas tree. But she is candid in the memoir about his frequent beatings of his children and most prolifically his wife. Viola and her older sister Deloris would escape the trauma of 'our mom being beaten and screaming in pain' by acting out role plays of being 'rich, white Beverly Hills matrons, with big jewels and little Chihuahuas'.

Her mother still bears the scars of the abuse, which might involve being stabbed in the leg or neck with a pencil, or being chased through the neighbourhood bloodied and fleeing for her life, leaving a trail of blood leading up to the front door. Davis writes: 'Sometimes her head or arm would be split open. She would have a swollen face, split lip. I was always afraid when he picked anything up like a piece of wood because he would hit her as hard as he could and keep beating. Sometimes all night.'

Dan Davis died of pancreatic cancer in 2006, having softened later in life into an adoring, apologetic husband and shelterer of struggling relatives, fellow addicts among them. He is the memoir's great story of redemption, depicted bedridden in his kitchen near the end of his life, weighing eighty-six pounds and calling for Mae Alice, asking repeatedly for forgiveness, a state of prostration and submission that Davis believes not everyone is capable of, 'I give him big props for that.' She herself is forgiving, exposing her father as abuser and perpetrator, while acknowledging his imprisonment in a system of historic racial and economic oppression that maimed him. 'I think that at some point, I had to make a choice – to see my father as just a demon or monster, or to see him as a man, as a man who's fighting who knows what kind of secrets, what kind of abuse, what kind of trauma. This is how we worked it out. Do I want to love my dad and have a relationship with him, or not? And I chose to want my father. And I think he chose us too.' When asked if she would have published his portrayal in *Finding Me* if he were still alive, she says resolutely that she would.

Davis is equally frank about the ubiquity of sexual abuse in her home and neighbourhood while growing up, with her and her sisters being subjected to offences from a relative as well as random perverts and paedophiles lurking in shops and other people's houses. On the set of *How To Get Away With Murder*, she worked with her long-time idol and original inspiration for

wanting to be an actor, Cicely Tyson, and recalls her saying
during a discussion about sexual assault: 'It happened to all the
women, that's our curse. It happened to my mother. It happened to her mother.' Part of Davis's intention in addressing it
in the memoir is to work against any tendency to downplay
sexual abuse as anything but a crime and, in exposing the truth
of what she saw and experienced, to give others permission and
courage to do the same. 'I'm fifty-six,' she says, 'and most of the
women I have met in my life – and I've met a lot of people –
have been sexually abused. You can tell through their behaviour,
in the partners they choose, in the way they communicate, the
way they hold themselves. It's almost like the secret that slowly
bleeds out, even when you're trying to hold it back and you're
putting Band-Aids on it. Secrets are destructive. They're a side-
effect of shame and trauma, and they make the abuser and the
oppressor very happy. And really, not to sound egotistical or
godlike, but I do feel like I have a job on this planet, in this life,
to make people feel less alone.'

Unlike many female actors, Davis has not fallen prey to the
culture of sexual abuse in Hollywood that accelerated the
#MeToo movement, but she is keen to point out the reality of
'deprivation' that characterises the industry, which predators
take full advantage of. Around 90 per cent of actors are
unemployed, and only 2 per cent earn enough to live on. As a
black woman entering the profession in the 1990s, her chances
of success were even slimmer, and she quickly became aware of
the double affront of racism and colourism, the scenario that in
order to succeed 'you either have to be a black female version of
a white ideal, or you have to be white'. After graduating from
Rhode Island College a theatre major, she was accepted into the
prestigious Juilliard School, of which she is critical for its crushing white-centrism, its desire to create the 'perfect white actor',
'something devoid of joy but steeped in technique'. 'There is no

set rule to how a character should be played,' she tells me emphatically. 'That was my issue with Juilliard. Whatever character I play, I'm not gonna play with the same palette as my white counterparts, because I'm different. My voice is different. Who I am is different. It was like, "Your voice is too deep, you're too hard. So you have to be light, but you have to be light like a ninety-pound white girl, you can't be *your* light" . . . I think that sometimes, everything that you are can crumble under the weight of Eurocentric and white-centric notions. There's nowhere for someone like me to go – nowhere. I mean, I got [a] wide nose, big lips, dark skin – where do I go? Look at me – I might as well walk through the doors of Juilliard and walk my ass out!'

Davis was forty-two when she landed the role as Mrs Miller in the film adaptation of John Patrick Shanley's play *Doubt*, alongside Meryl Streep and Phillip Seymour Hoffman, an eight-minute performance entailing two weeks' work that garnered her first Oscar nomination and marked her passage from stage actor to screen and Hollywood. She had already received the Tony Award for *King Hedley II*, but had struggled with her TV and film credits. Many of the characters she fit the description for in casting were drug-addicted mothers, and she recalls that the 'pretty' or sexualised roles were never given to her, even when the producers were black. She played a 'huge slate' of 'best friends to white women', along with a host of authoritarian cops and FBI agents. Leading parts continued to elude her even after *Time* magazine named her one of the 100 Most Influential People in the World in 2012. Her first TV lead, in *How To Get Away With Murder*, came from African American-led production company Shondaland, as defence attorney and law professor Annalise Keating, a liberating role in which she was finally allowed to play the character of an ordinary, complex woman.

She accepted the job on the condition that she be allowed to take off her wig in the first season, which she saw as a way of honouring black women 'by not showing an image that is palatable to the oppressor'.

It is this focus on the human story, beyond the reductive stereotypes, that Davis believes will mark real progression in the fight for greater diversity in the acting industry. We should arrive at a place 'where the show is just the human being and the human event. It's not you being a metaphor for a larger social issue. It's not you going to a movie theatre and walking out going, "What did it *mean* for that black man to be in that role? What do you think they were ultimately *saying*?" I feel that as soon as we move away from metaphoric land and get into the land where people put their butts in the seat and their only investment is to follow you through your story, that's when we will have really changed. You don't have to be crying over your dead son's body that's just been killed in a drive-by shooting for your emotions to be valuable.' And the realising of this utopia is not in the hands of the perennially white male gatekeepers who hold most of the power to bring projects to fruition, but of artists of colour like herself who are creating material for themselves and people who look like them – Issa Rae, Michaela Coel, Octavia Spencer, Taraji P. Henson, Kerry Washington, Regina King, Gabrielle Union. 'They're waking up to ownership. They're waking up to agency and autonomy. All of us now are saying No, we're not waiting, we're gonna be the change we wanna see.'

Davis and Julius set up JuVee Productions in 2011 for exactly this reason, to create their own roles and narratives with the aim of broadening the public perception of African American lives. That's not to say, though, that every role does not still come with its own portion of anxiety. She is 'terrified' about what Michelle Obama will think of her portrayal of her in *The First*

Lady. In preparation, she watched the documentary *Becoming* at least twenty-two times and listened to over a hundred of her podcasts (which she adores), as well as spending time with Obama and reading her and her husband's books. What surprised her most in her research was the simple matter of well-being. 'Here's the thing about Michelle Obama, which is very different from me, different from a lot of people: she's healthy. She's a healthy human being, because she grew up in an environment where she always felt seen, always felt worthy. Maybe because I've been with a lot of artists in my life, a lot of people who've been traumatised, including myself, it's very interesting to portray someone who literally is healthy.' Her favourite role of all, she says, was playing James Brown's mother in *Get On Up* alongside the late Chadwick Boseman, whose final role was in *Ma Rainey's Black Bottom*. 'I enjoyed being in Mississippi. I loved Chadwick, *loved* Chadwick. It was sort of awesome.'

Despite the obstacles it has placed in her way, Davis describes the acting profession as 'a healing wellspring', allowing her to both meet and escape herself, alongside other balms she has drawn on in her transformative life, such as therapy, friends, teachers and spirit guides, a loving family, and Jacuzzi time with her husband. She is, ultimately, a survivor, while inherently rejecting the stereotypical use of that word in relation to black women. She wants us all to survive, so she has shown us all of herself, the low self-esteem, the fretful overachieving, the fibroids and alopecia, the feeling of never being enough. In finding herself, she points a way, holds a light, for others. 'In order to break generational curses, you have to become aware yourself, accountable yourself, and share your stories to the generation coming behind you,' she says from her vantage point at the top of her game, where she remembers amid the noise to savour the quiet moments. The quiet is where who we are takes place, and she is no longer running away. 'I think that's one of the reasons why we work so hard. I think it's motivated by trauma, and it's motivated by the fact that if we stop, then somehow we're not worthy. That's not *true*. You're worthy. You were worthy when you were born.'

Guardian, 2022

Once a Dancer

One cold, dark Monday night in a March of my midlife, in that moment of winter when spring wants to hold on just a little longer before arriving, I travelled across London to a bathhouse basement in King's Cross to learn the dance routine to Beyoncé's 'Single Ladies'. The basement was part of an establishment called Drink, Shop & Do, and like several feelgood, eclectic pop-ups founded by twenty-first-century entrepreneurs, it no longer exists post-pandemic. The idea was that one might wander in from the urban concourse and hang out in the bright-toned café, maybe browse for a while the gift cards or jewellery on sale in a corner, and then, if the mood takes you, or indeed if you have come especially, you could venture downstairs to the bare floor and the waiting music to get your freak on. There were many other activities offered under 'Do', as I recall, such as candle making, Lego robot construction and tea towel screen-printing. It was a nice concept, just flimsy in the face of a plague.

We gathered, us women – there were no men – in the subterranean dim, shyly at the edges, apart from the usual one or two dance-class regulars who know the moves or each other or the teacher or just don't mind being up front and visible while shaking it. We set down our bags by the wall and took off our coats. We were wearing leggings and fluorescent trainers, sports bras, scrunchies and ventilated T-shirts, and all of us wanted to move like Beyoncé in that monumental black-and-white video of 2008, while at the same time remaining respectfully aware that we would not. She was a recurrent theme at Drink Shop & Do, her slew of hits headlining many a dance class here – 'Crazy in

Love', 'Run the World' – sometimes she even made a personal appearance (via an impersonator). Her dexterous, swift-footed routines were taught by resident dance teacher Jemima Bloom, whose repertoire also included tango, belly dancing, flamenco and other styles.

At that time I was missing dancing. It's a feeling that still comes over me, the need to stretch, leap, shake, flex, snap, flicker, shimmy, mosey, step, strut and swipe in an open space with the air zipping past my face and music surrounding, directing. To lose control in a melody. To be fast and in flight, in so doing, to escape the world. Having changed occupations from dancing to writing some years earlier, thus now being a person who spent much of the working day in a chair where once I had been on my feet, in motion, I missed the abandon and swirl of the theatrical life, the waking up of a morning to the prospect of consistent, purposeful movement. And so I went to a class sometimes. I had tried African, Afro-Cuban, Caribbean, jazz, contemporary, African contemporary. I had been to The Place in Euston, Pineapple Dance Studios in Covent Garden, to the IRIE! dance theatre headquarters in Deptford to try a reggae-fusion style, all in an effort to retaliate against my swivel chair and reconnect with flight. But it never quite worked to fill the movement void. It was never quite high enough. I was an outsider now, had conceded to gravity.

In the corner of the Drink, Shop & Do basement was a battered old grand piano next to a few stacks of plastic chairs. On the wall were five glittery, jumpy silver letters saying DANCE! Having set up her music system, Jemima announced that it was time, whereupon the majority of us positioned ourselves as close to the back row as possible, away from the accusatory frontal mirrors. It can put you off your steps, glimpsing yourself fluffing the routine or struggling to keep up, getting a sense of what your body looks like in relation to other bodies, so helplessly loaded are our brains with the admonitions of body fascism. The attendees at the front of the dance floor are watched from behind as exemplars, demonstrators, and for a routine as complicated as 'Single Ladies', they would be referred to here with the utmost need and intensity. Street dance is hard. Of all the styles I've tried it's the one I've found the most difficult. There is so much intricately timed coordination required, with the snapping of the head and the pumping of an arm and then the mathematics of the feet, hands and hips. Every time I've tried street dance I've felt like a marionette under the manoeuvre of a mismatched puppeteer – as cool as it looks in the videos, it's not my natural language.

Jemima did that thing, though, where the teacher divides the group into two and makes them perform the routine to each other, so in this class there was no hiding. After a thorough cardiovascular warm-up involving running on the spot to Maroon 5, army-style knee-ups and some killer abs exercises that left us panting for less, she took us through the hallowed choreography (originally inspired by a 1969 Bob Fosse routine), from the wrist-dropping two-step at the beginning to the jaunty circular strut and gyrating lunge, the specific dips and turns. It was quite stunning amid the heat and challenge of the situation to think that this routine is usually delivered in heels, that most of Beyoncé's high-octane performances are given in a beautification assemblage involving stilettos, flapping hair extensions and very little ankle support – how does she *do* it! how do those ladies *balance*! We were inadequate, humbled by their spectacular prowess. During our group performances there were squeals of embarrassment and face-hiding shame. We persevered for the full two hours, which, it turns out, is not much time for a class of amateurs to learn a professional dance routine; we had to rush through the last few moves and our finales were shabby, flawed and floundering. A sad thing was that in no way, not at any point, did I stand out as someone who knew a thing or two about dance.

My first grown-up dancing lessons took place in a community hall in Moulsecoomb, on the A270 towards Lewes. There, I had been chosen. I had been walking through my university campus one bright blue afternoon, and a stocky, warm-eyed South African man came up to me and asked if I was interested in being in a dance company. I was, kind of. I carried around a vision of myself dancing on an outdoor stage at a Maltese auditorium, next to a set of DJ decks. When I listened to soukous or R&B, for example, I saw its dancing in my head, like an extra bass or layer of sound, or an internal music video. As teenagers three friends and I had choreographed and performed a dance routine to Michael Jackson's 'P.Y.T.' I regularly went to the Zap or the Beachcomber nightclubs on Brighton's seafront and shocked out all night to house or disco, sometimes on the stage, and I would often find myself breaking out into random jigging in the middle of a conversation or family gathering when a fine song sailed in on the airwaves. Why wouldn't I be interested in joining a dance company? So I 'auditioned', was 'chosen' (there wasn't exactly a lot of competition, it must be said; to an extent, we had already been chosen – the audition was more to check that we were trainable).

Our talent scout, dance instructor and artistic director proceeded to teach his newly assembled troupe traditional dances from South Africa, from West Africa, from the Caribbean. After a day spent in the library studying audiovisual analysis or the politics of representation in the British press, I went to Moulsecoomb and learned the Kpanlogo of Ghana, the mask dances of Senegal, the gumboot dance of South Africa, performed by goldmine workers during the apartheid era. Light would fall in from the large windows like an enfolding lace. An array of teachers and instructors were brought in to show us the Kumina dances from Jamaica (via Congo), the Bata of Nigeria and the Vodú moves of Cuba, so that we might deliver them anew, preserving cultures with our bodies. We shared special moments of corporal endeavour and spiritual, world-expanding fulfilment. We practised and practised. Martha Graham wrote once that the activity of practice, be it in dancing or living, can lead to the 'shape of achievement, a sense of one's being, a satisfaction of spirit. One becomes, in some area, an athlete of God.'[4] It did at times feel like a training and an adventure of divine proportions to be present in that slanting-ceilinged hall, sweating and stepping to the djembe pops and the call of the elegant hollow congas.

Our director had a plan, to bring African and Caribbean dance to the peoples of southeast England and possibly beyond, starting with Brighton, and for a while he succeeded. Our first performance was at a seafront pub-cum-club called the Volks Tavern, where I forgot most of the steps out of stage fright. It got easier. I realised that an audience notices less than you think. I learned to 'style it out'. We performed in little summer festivals, then in bigger ones. We did WOMAD. We were the run-up act there for South African percussion ensemble Amampondo, and went up on stage in a huge tent containing thousands of cheering, tipsy spectators. We felt at times groupie-susceptible. I had a passing flirtation with reggae singjay Eek-A-Mouse after his gig at my university, which had nothing to do with the dance troupe but I reasoned that there had to be a showbiz link. As part of his masterplan, our director got together an entire dance theatre production in which I played the lead part, and this toured for a while in theatres and other large tents. We had a tour schedule. We performed at the Edinburgh Festival and London's South Bank. Once, we gave a show in Victoria Embankment Gardens by the Thames – we had made it to the West End.

The 1990s were an exciting time for black dance forms in Britain.[5] There was a proliferation of companies and troupes bringing movement modes from all over the black and brown continents and across the diaspora, the largest and most success-ful of these Adzido Pan African Dance Ensemble, founded in 1984 by Ghanaian dancer and choreographer George Dzikunu, the first black dance company to receive fixed-term funding from the Arts Council. Kokuma Dance Theatre Company was another longstanding traditionalist troupe, initially focusing on creative African dance then gradually shifting towards Carib-bean dance via collaboration with Jamaican practitioners Jackie Guy and H Patten. Following in the footsteps of pioneering fusionist troupes like MAAS Movers and Union Dance, there were dynamic dance innovators fusing traditional vocabularies with contemporary lines, such as Bode Lawal's Sakoba Dance Theatre, Beverley Glean's IRIE! Dance Theatre and Peter Badejo's equally well-established Badejo Arts, which tackled themes of migration and black subjectivity through dance. Former Rambert dancer Sheron Wray founded her company JazzXchange in 1992, her repertoire a fusion of jazz, classical and street styles, while MC and choreopoet Jonzi D merged hip-hop and dance theatre in his 1995 production *Lyrikal Fearta*, a precursor to *The Aeroplane Man*, all of this activity steadily building towards the staging of the first Black British Dance Festival in 1997. It was a scene full of such passion, excitement and substance that I became convinced, in the futile design of hindsight, that I had made the wrong choice of degree subject: I should have been studying Choreography and Spanish at Mid-dlesex, or Dance Therapy at Hertfordshire, or IRIE!'s pioneering Diploma in African and Caribbean Dance, the first course of its kind in Europe.

Instead, having finished my now-regrettable academic degree and moving back into my childhood bedroom in London, where

I wondered how I was ever going to afford my own place while waitressing at Chiquito, I took off to Cuba for two months with a couple of friends to take a course in Afro-Cuban dance. We stayed with a Cuban family in Guantanamo Bay, by day learning the dances of the Yoruba Orishas – the majestic, flowy blue sweeps of Yemaya the ocean goddess, the charging, stormy ferocity of Shango, god of lightning and thunder – which I imagined I might bring back to the London scene and blend into some profoundly original choreography. We travelled east to Baracoa on a rickety bus lurching towards the cliff edge, then west to Santiago de Cuba, learned more dances, ate *yuca con mojo* in the *paladares*. By the time we got up to Havana, though, my two friends were missing their boyfriends. They sighed and slumped with longing. I found them disappointing in their loved-up helplessness. 'We are in CUBA,' I said. 'We are actually in HAVANA.' But they just wanted to go home. They changed their flights and left me there, after which I spent long afternoons walking up and down the Malecón alone, watching the chopping waves and the curly drifting foam as it dipped and turned with the tide.

When I tell people that I used to be a dancer, it seems only half a truth. I was never officially trained. I went to no Laban, conservatoire or Rambert. I sidestepped into it, rode its fairground waltzer for a while and then I went and got a desk job. I can't imagine, now, getting up on stage in a swaying Xhangani skirt and African Dutch wax headwrap and mentoing to live percussion, or screeching or ululating in accompaniment as we used to at the heights of beats. Time has passed. Life itself has moved. Now much of my dancing is internal, still in my head inside of music, and also, I tend to think, inside of sentences, the rhythms of language, in the movements made possible with words. Otherwise, 'my body became increasingly strange to me', as

Lorrie Moore once wrote in a short story ('Strings Too Short to Use') that comes to mind. 'I became very aware of its edges as I peered out from it: my shoulders, hands, strands of hair.'

After Cuba I was still doing shifts at Chiquito (balancing cornflaked ice-cream desserts and sizzling fajitas on a large oval tray) and, approaching my mid-twenties, I realised that I needed to make a major career decision. Was I going to devote myself to a life in dance with all its hardship, instability, crushing auditions and infrequent waitress-doubled employment, or was I going to follow my penchant for writing and try for a job in journalism? I chose the latter, my hand forced by another audition failure, this one in Brixton Hill where I performed a humiliating solo improvisation during which I sensed that an ending was nigh. Whereas before it had seemed that the black dance world was a thriving metropolis of enthralment, travel, enrichment, spiritual connection and fulfilment, now it seemed just basically impossible to get a gig or make some money to buy a sandwich. Troupes were struggling to survive. Funding was fading. The already-fragile fringe dance infrastructure was coming undone in the beginning of the political slaying of the creative arts, and the Brighton ensemble had all but disbanded. Perhaps, after all, my degree choice had not been so misjudged. It was as though my dancer path had meandered away beyond the Malecón wall into the waves of the Atlantic – I had left it behind in Cuba.

What happens to a dancer when they stop dancing? What happens in the soul? This was a question I became preoccupied with post-troupe, during the subsequent writing of a novel that I never imagined I would want to write, having been a (kind of) dancer: a novel about dancing, an encapsulation of its nature. I had thought of writing and dancing as opposing creative callings. I had thought it would be pointless and purely nostalgic to try to bring the two together in a book. But the urge surfaced, maybe as a symptom of missing dancing, plus I had been doing some reviewing of the London performances, scribbling the spectacle in the dark and sending in my copy the next morning. Delving into the history of black dancers in Britain, I became aware of the Jamaican dancer and choreographer Berto Pasuka, who along with fellow Jamaican Richie Riley founded Les Ballet Nègres in 1946, blending classical training with African and Caribbean cultures and taking Europe by storm. The company was such a sensation that one Amsterdam audience had to be spread into the orchestra pit due to high demand, and at the height of their fame they were only performing in first-class theatres and opera houses. Without established funding, though, they survived just six years. In 1963 Pasuka was mysteriously found dead in his home, for which no explanation has ever been found. This story stayed with me and sparked my imagination. I began to read biographies of other dancers. I read about the lives of Alvin Ailey, Lucia Joyce and Vaslav Nijinsky, and what recurred in these life stories was the common theme of mental malaise, an unravelling in periods of dormancy or after-dance, the dangerous misery of motionlessness. They (we?) were fallen beings, descended from realms ethereal into the madness of ordinary life. Or, in some cases, the after-dance exacerbated an instability that was already there and had previously been carried in the wings of flight. I wonder also if it is that dancers exist in a retained, physical state of childhood, and when they no longer dance they are met with the sharp impurity of adulthood.

In each book I have written, there has emerged along the way a particular object of (usually historical) fascination. These have included the moving of the original 'crystal palace' from Hyde Park to the Penge Place estate in 1854 after the Great Exhibition, and Victorian Prime Minister William Gladstone's weekend retreats at Dollis Hill House in Gladstone Park in northwest London. When this happens, it means that the creative process is going well, because it is alive around you, sprouting tendrils, even if temporarily destabilised by these tendrils. For a time while writing the novel about dancing – entitled *The Wonder* – I again became obsessed, this time with the Russian ballet dancer Vaslav Nijinsky. I was taken with his early muteness, his legendary superhuman leap, the story of how he was dismissed from Sergei Diaghilev's Ballets Russes on his marriage to the daughter of a Hungarian count. Thrown as a teenager into a world of glamour and wild adulation, subsequent mental breakdown and schizophrenia were eventually met with a long medical feast of neuroleptics, morphine, opium, scopolamine, bromides, barbiturates, insulin and straitjackets.[6] The ghost of him haunted my pages with a strange and far-back darkness, a spoiled 'athlete of God', coughing from insulin. He makes a cameo in the novel's final scene, in the form of an apparition, marking the protagonist's arrival at oblivion. The obsession had found a meaning inside the story it had punctured, which it must; everything in a story must have purpose, in order for it to belong.

The writing of *The Wonder* acted as a necessary bridge towards a post-dancing life. On a wall in my house now, there is a black-and-white photograph of Nijinsky, dressed in costume for his ballet *The Afternoon of a Faun*. There is another picture of Katherine Dunham leaning against a pillar with a ribbon in her hair (she also makes an appearance in the novel). At times I imagine Vaslav walking out of his outline into Katherine's, and together they perform a breathtaking duet from the beyond of their necropolis. The weaving together through sentences of a narrative in which these dancing lives could be glimpsed and re-enacted ultimately enabled another kind of internal, cerebral flying, in which I could conjure the magic gloom of an empty theatre, the silent stage wings, a bus sloping along a Jamaican mountainside containing a little boy who wants to be a dancer, and most of all the delicious feeling of movement itself, that fevered writing of oneself across the air.

At the end of the Drink, Shop & Do 'Single Ladies' class, Jemima Bloom played a relaxing Romain Virgo song called 'Love Doctor' and we did our warm-down. We stretched and lunged, lay on the bathhouse basement floor in states of exhaustion, in full acceptance of our humility in the face of Queen Bey. As the warm reggae chords drifted up and down over our aching abdominals and shaken limbs, I was thankful for the way dancing can return you to your own body, whichever language the choreography is written in. Jemima told us to breathe deeply in and out. We stood and brought our arms up over our heads and then let them float down again. Three months later I tried ballet, a few months after that couples' salsa, and more recently an eighties student nightclub in Brighton where they played Madonna and Chico DeBarge's 'Rhythm of the Night'. Dancing is good for us. According to psychologists, a thorough get-down in your local club once a week has a positive effect on the cerebellum. I am working on this utopia. I am looking for a local place that plays the right music. Once a dancer, always a dancer.

Granta, 2023

Writers, Writing

A Meeting with Alice Walker

Transatlantic interviews often take place in the evening, because of the time difference, so a journalist might find herself alone in the office, talking to her subject on the phone. The others have all left for the day, down the spiral stairs, the room has taken on the quiet of surrounding darkness. The monitors, the fax machine are switched off and beams of street light coming through the windows are spread across the desks, the sound of traffic passing by outside on Battersea Bridge Road. The voice on the end of the line is that of Alice Walker, of whom I have been a long-time reader and enthusiast. There was some scepticism from my senior colleagues about whether I was the best person for this feature – they were concerned that I would lack objectivity, drench her impression in schmaltz. I was allowed to do it on the condition that I exercise my most steely professional distance.

I prepared thoroughly, reading the press material, reading beyond and around it, gathering questions, finding entrances into avenues of dialogue. I made sure I had a fresh cassette tape, free of any prior voice, that the recorder would not run out of batteries and that the connections to the handset were secure. Nervously I determined to be steely, to keep a proper detachment. As the interview ran its course, though, what I found was that it is difficult to be steely when disarmed by someone. She radiated an expansive stillness. There was a kind of old pain and kindness in her voice. About halfway through the interview, she stopped mid-sentence and asked, 'What's wrong? You don't sound happy.' It was such a sudden and frank question that I could only answer honestly, and told her that I had recently lost someone to suicide. A brief silence, and we talked for a while about this. I asked her what she would have told this person I had lost if she could have spoken to her before the fatal decision. 'I would have told her to hold on,' she said, 'until it passes. Everything passes.'

I remember this advice in times of necessity. It has been very useful to me. A few weeks after our interview, Alice came to London on a book tour, and I went to see her speak at the Broadway Theatre in Catford. She held the room with her gentle presence. She talked about how long it had taken her to build the sense of comfort in public to address a crowd without a script. There was a long queue of people waiting for book signings at the end. Up close, she had an aura, a shine, a sense of great and ancient self-protection. I thanked her for her empathy in noticing and giving time to the vulnerability of a stranger. The article was published in the summer of 1998, when I was still a new journalist, and although I had a lot to learn, there is a simplicity to the conversation that I find valuable. I'm sure that what she says about 'a great vision' had a hand in the initial inspiration to write my first novel, *26a*. She also talked about the importance, in order to write, of living the person who you are, and the work is nourished and made possible that way. She remains a crucial reference point to so many of us when we are lost in the wilderness. I pick up *In Search of Our Mother's Gardens*, or *The Temple of My Familiar*, and remember the earth beneath my feet.

★

Alice Walker believes we can change the world. She's spent roughly half a century working on it, through her novels, short stories, essays, poetry and memoirs, as well as grassroots activism addressing such things as capitalist exploitation, racism, gender inequality, female genital mutilation and climate abuse. Those problems that she can't tackle, she spends whole nights worrying about.

She has been described as someone who 'writes like an angel'. She writes, she says, 'to make myself well'. In 1996 she published her memoir, *The Same River Twice: Honouring the Difficult*, which explored her transition from being a solitary writer with a very loud story (*The Color Purple*) to a public figure with a quiet demeanour. Her written response to calls to ban Steven Spielberg's movie adaptation of *The Color Purple* on account of the novel's controversial material was, 'Why don't they ban nuclear power?' The novel won the Pulitzer Prize in 1983.

'I think that women have been sitting on their feelings and their thoughts for thousands of years and it's high time they started expressing themselves,' she declares. Conversing with Alice Walker is a paradoxical experience. Here is someone whose books have become virtual bibles for oppressed people around the world. Someone who takes it upon herself to scold presidents, disprove propaganda, challenge tradition. Yet the humility and ease of her personality give a sense that you could be talking to a member of your own family. She dismisses her own importance. 'I don't see myself as a role model, and I would basically not advocate role-model thought. What is valuable about people always is that they are exactly who they are – and that's invigorating; it's joyful.'

She was born in the segregated Southern state of Georgia, to Minnie Tallulah Grant and her sharecropper husband, Willie Lee Walker. The youngest of eight children, she lived with her siblings in a ramshackle house where the family struggled to make ends meet. 'I was very much someone who was probably never expected to be heard from at all,' she says. As a child she communicated with spirits on her back porch, and this innate mental and emotional transcendence was to become the foundation for her literature, which often features stunningly visual dreamscapes alongside a reverence towards the healing powers of nature. Her characters are not 'made up'; they are actual souls who present themselves through her open door, and make her acquaintance. So enduring is her awareness of the spirit world that she has become something of a mystic – 'Madame Walker', as she is known to her tarot-reading punters. Sometimes she carries a magic wand. She allows herself only two hours of TV a week and encourages me not to read newspapers and magazines.

Walker tells me that her fourth novel, *The Temple of My Familiar* (1989), was the result of a 'phenomenal spiritual vision', the manifestation of which took her three years to complete. It reads like a kaleidoscope. There is a celestial quality to its pages. According to a Native American shaman, she explains, 'in every human life, there comes a time when you have a great vision. It's about how it all connects – all life, you know – the present, the future, the plants, the animals, people, everything. That comes to you, it's a natural thing . . . if you're open to it. And that's basically what happened to me. So at that point, the only thing you have to do is to manifest it for the people. And that is usually where people fall short.' It is precisely her disconnection from what is artificial that has enabled her to achieve the depth of thought at work in her writing. Though she insists, 'I am an Earthling. I am here.'

From conservative quarters, Walker has had her fair share of scepticism over the years on account of her deepening and wholehearted espousal of all things spiritual. She has been accused of shamanism, hippiedom, Buddhism, of referring to people too often as 'flowers'. Certainly, her brand of black womanism (as opposed to feminism, a movement that tended to exclude black women) has become less fashionable, yet her writing remains languid and effortlessly graceful, and has not lost its enormous power to prod at the sorest, most critical anxieties of the human condition. While her more recent writing may seem preoccupied with an ethereal inner world, the suggestion emerges from it that a reassessment and realignment of the self is an effective contribution to our surrounding dystopia.

Her collection of essays, *Anything We Love Can Be Saved*, offers generous insights into her very private existence – what colour she painted her front door, details of her crockery and nightwear. One American critic described it as 'so personal as to be uninteresting'. But that's missing the point. 'These are all messages to myself to celebrate life as I express it in my own body and my own being, in my perception of what is wonderful. This is enough of a colourless, dead, impersonal world – people who want that, they can have it, but I'm sick of it and I will have no more of it in my personal life. That's the point. I'm optimistic about my own ability to be a better person every day, to make the effort.'

Of her activism, the film *Warrior Marks* (1994), which Walker made with her friend Pratibha Parmar, is among her most impactful efforts, drawing attention to the trauma of female genital mutilation. She has also visited AIDS sufferers in Cuba – where she found that they were receiving advice, care and rehabilitation, contrary to the popular anti-Castro spin – and she makes a habit of getting involved and taking a stand wherever she feels it could help. 'Everything. Everything needs to be done in every movement,' she says. 'It's about time running out for the planet and people needing to wake up to their responsibilities, however small they feel they are in the face of them – just contribute, contribute your insight, your view, your joy, your sorrow. Just put it all out there and hope that people can take hold of what we have left and try to preserve it; not so much for their generation, but just out of respect for having been here at all.'

A creature of magic she may be, but hers is no wonderland, and she carries her wand as a method of personal as well as collective survival. If she did ever stop writing, she imagines that instead she would become a 'wandering inspiration', walking through the mess of humanity in an attempt to make it well. 'I love writing,' she says, 'and I've tried to retire from it many times. But there's a joy in it that is just exactly that feeling of spring rising in you and this is how you express your life. So it's not something I can easily leave.' Whether we lean towards cynicism or hope, and whether or not the bulk of her work is done, Alice Walker is one of the fundamental visionaries of our time, the relevance of her message increasing, rather than decreasing, the further we descend into trouble.

Pride, 1998

Five Minutes with Maya Angelou

'Get out! Get back, stop it, stop it, stop it!' Maya Angelou is
addressing an opportune photographer, who promptly scuttles
away. She is standing on stage at The Dorchester wearing a sassy
black dress and cracking poetic jokes. This is the speech everyone in attendance at her £80-a-ticket seventieth birthday party
has been waiting for. Preceded by a series of impassioned trib-
utes (such as Paul Boateng's vociferous 'Daughter of Africa!'), it
came time for the lady herself to stand before us. Poet that she
is, she got heads nodding in affirmation, murmurs of agreement,
a collective adoring gaze, and most of all laughter. 'I don't trust
people who don't laugh,' she professed. 'I don't trust people
who don't love themselves.'

Born on 4 April 1928 in Missouri, USA, named Marguerite
Johnson by her parents but nicknamed 'Baker Nigger' by local
bigots because she worked in a bakery, Angelou was abused at an
early age by a male relative and, in response, decided not to
speak for six years. Shakespeare and Langston Hughes brought
her back: 'Poetry can be a saviour,' she says. 'It has been for me,
particularly in the silent years.' A teenage pregnancy resulted in
the birth of her son, and she eventually turned to prostitution in
an attempt to alleviate grinding poverty.

Now, she is the celebrated author of twenty-one books, a
revered civil-rights activist, ambassador, benefactor and holder
of fifty-two honorary degrees. Her experiences, good and bad,
are chronicled in five autobiographical novels, the first volume
of which, *I Know Why the Caged Bird Sings* (1969), has sold several
million copies worldwide. Nearly three decades later she's in

London celebrating her birthday and raising money for the NSPCC (National Society for the Prevention of Cruelty to Children), checking on her own child-protection project, The Maya Angelou Family Centre, and 'beating the drum' for a new book, *Even the Stars Look Lonesome*, a collection of essays on 'what it is like to be human, and American, what makes us weep, what makes us fall and stumble and somehow rise again and go on from darkness into darkness'.

Her home-from-home in London is the Basil Street Hotel, and for our meeting earlier that day she was forgivably late, her broad, six-foot frame looming over her entourage. Black suit, full-length skirt, red lipstick, a huge, multicoloured velvet hat. By then she was tired, lacking the energy for yet another interview. 'Five minutes,' she warned in her thick, masculine drawl. She is moist-eyed, a pearl necklace at her throat. Her face is monumental.

In 1993, Maya Angelou was commissioned to write and recite a poem for Bill Clinton's inauguration. She read 'On the Pulse of Morning'. But did she trust him? 'Of course,' she begins, surprised by the question. 'I mean, no . . . and yes.' She lets out a sudden laugh, her gapped front teeth and wide mouth in full glory. 'If I trusted them entirely, I'd stop voting, and cease talking. I have a lot to fight for. I feel very sorry for people who have no raison d'être, no reason to be, nothing to fight for. I have a lot to struggle against, to beat the drum for . . . So, I like my government.'

The civil-rights movement that Angelou participated in alongside Martin Luther King may have triumphed in many ways, but much has been lost since then. With a regal and dramatic gesture, she laments a past togetherness. 'We've gained something, but we've lost some sense of community. When a whole people are under the hammer they tend to pull together. But if the hammer is lifted, sometimes the group that has a little money goes over there, the group that has a little art goes over there, the group that has a little duty goes over there. And so we become fractured.'

Starting out as a singer and dancer, touring with an opera production of *Porgy and Bess*, after her work in the civil-rights movement Angelou married a South African activist and eventually ended up in Cairo, then Ghana, as the first female editor of *The Arab Observer*. Of the time she spent living in Africa, she recalls, 'I relearned what I always knew, the way we really learn things. I remembered that what I thought had been created in the US – the morals and methods of our living – really were African in the first place.' And then her famous assertion: 'What I remembered was that human beings are more alike than unalike. If you can ingest the least bit of that,' she says, 'it means that all the wisdom in the world belongs to you.'

Even in her seventieth year, Maya Angelou is still fiercely devoted to her people and her causes. At the same time she is a true glamour queen, who will dance on until this life is over. How does she feel about death? She raises her brow, considers for a moment. 'Well, so many different things. I'm relieved that I have it to look forward to. I wouldn't like to be here forever.' Another majestic smile and she concludes, 'I'm keen to live with courage and laughter. I'm also keen to die with grace. I want to have lived so that I've made life a little better for you, that you've learned something about living this exquisite experiment.'

Fifteen minutes have gone by. The Dorchester was waiting.

Pride, 1998

Jean Rhys and the Charisma of Despair

I never intended to be a writer. I began writing in a journal, at around fifteen years old, when the world seemed wide and unfathomable, full of rising questions. To try to address the questions, to figure out what I was seeing and experiencing, I wrote. There were revelations, dreams, confessions, confusions. Writing them down helped me feel more rooted and present in the world and able to participate in it, on the foundation of a necessary self-connection. It has always been like that. When some time has passed in which I have not written, there is instability and a sense of flailing. That is the simple answer to the recurring question (from readers, from random fellow passengers on planes) of why I write. It enables me to exist in the world.

Another question I am often asked is *how* I write. There is the more practical, physical dimension to this question concerning pen versus keyboard and Mac versus PC etc., which is easy and dull to answer (I write on a PC with no internet connection, at a corner desk in an upstairs room). The other dimension is more confounding, because it is something I am always asking myself while trying to write: How is it done? How was it done last time? Can it, *should* it, be done again? I am not always sure that the person asking the question was interested in this second dimension, whose answer is usually meandering, involving accounts of brainstorming sessions, futile planning, drafting and temporary abandonments. Writing, though it comes so naturally to me, has also been distressingly difficult in every attempt I've made to render it into the short story or the novel, which are the two literary forms to which I think I am most suited – the novel is a country to which I belong, the short story a region I dream of inhabiting, like a shimmering, still distant harbour.

There comes a point in any battle or bewilderment where a person acquires comrades. Even in the solipsism of journal writing, I sensed that I was involved in a private yet, on some expansive level, communal activity. It was a feeling that grew as I got older, as the journal entries began leaning towards poetry, and I read the work of people who were actually writers, such as Jean Binta Breeze, Linton Kwesi Johnson, Oscar Allen (who was also a community activist and farmer, he lived in a small house at the top of a hill in a village in St Vincent, and he wrote once,

> perhaps the truth is more so that I am unhappy about myself and the times I am living in. I see myself as a creature of movements, belonging to the volcano, always stirring in the depths, planning to bring new material and new forms to the surface of the earth. But now I feel as if I am disconnected from the depths, cut loose from the magma, shrivelled up on the lawn, living in a foreign time,[7]

which I found recently in one of my notebooks, and it struck me, now that Oscar Allen is no longer alive, how writing facilitates a kind of immortality, an enduring voice, speaking through the ages, to be discovered at arbitrary moments and evoke an almost forgotten way of being and seeing). There was also, crucially, Alice Walker, and Toni Cade Bambara, and Toni Morrison, and those writers who were speaking from a corresponding perspective to my own, in that they understood the racial oppressions in which we lived and expressed an innate retaliation. Ali Smith, John Fowles, Richard Wright, Audre Lorde, Mark Doty, Rita Dove, Carol Shields. They were speaking to me from their islands of the mind, from where they were calling – Raymond Carver, Langston Hughes, Arundhati Roy. And then, of course, there was Jean Rhys.

Writing is a conversation. It is a canyon of perspectives, imagery, impressions, reactions, commentary on what is missing from what is being spoken, for example, or on how the same idea or premise might look from another angle. The writers who have angered me or made me impatient, because there is some careless omission in an impression of the world that they have created, have helped me as much as – if not more than – the writers who have inspired me through reflection or commonality. Sometimes, on reading a writer like John Updike or Richard Yates, the inspiration is in wishing to adjust a faulty lens, at the same time as wanting to convey a similar landscape view in my own territory. And there is also the situation where a voice, a particular, singular voice, feels so accurate, so honest in its way of seeing, that it is as if it is whispering to me, as I am walking through an airport, say, or waking in the morning, it lingers in my thoughts and has tied itself to them. It was like that on first reading James Salter. It's still like that with Jean Rhys.

I came across Jean Rhys while I was writing my first novel, *26a*. I had extracted myself from my perfectly bearable life in London to take the MA in Creative Writing at the University of East Anglia, and was living in a small room in a student house in Norwich, with a single bed, a single bookcase and a desk facing away from the window so that when I was writing my back was to the light. It was the last enclosure I had given myself in which to complete this book, requiring as it did an absolute and unwavering concentration, not least for my own mental well-being. For this was a very hard book to write. It was the breaking of me and the making of me, and what made it so difficult, what made it necessary to remove myself from my everyday reality, was the battle that needed to be fought between what I wanted to express and what I felt compromised in expressing – the battle between the story and the truth.

One evening, about four years earlier, I had been recently

bereaved by the death of the closest person in the world to me, my twin. We had entered life together, on the same day. When she died, the feeling was of such an intensity that it seemed that her spirit had inhabited my body, and on this particular evening during that strange time, when there was a glitter in the air and a new excruciating singularity (yet duality) of being, I was standing by the window in my living room, and I suddenly sat down on the sofa – the word, most accurately, is 'sank' – with the force of an idea. Dusk was moving into night. The sky was the magic colour when there are visitations, revelations. This, I realised, was what I wanted to express with the writing that had become my companion through my experiences. This precise feeling of inhabitation in mourning – and the whole story around it, the story of the loss but also the comfort of the knowledge that an absence is not absolute, that there are other, unexpected ways of being present, materialised by the people you have left behind.

Another question I often get asked, about *26a* specifically, is, Was it cathartic? This one makes me bristle a little. It appears to imply that the intention in crafting a story drawn from the personal is innately healing, and that the approach to doing so is self-serving, rather than an outward offering. In fact, there was nothing cathartic about it. From that moment on the sofa, when I began to think of the bereavement as a story to be told, it became necessary to postpone the progression of healing. In order to write about it, I had to look at it, put it up to the light, examine and dissect it, delve into its darkness and stay there for what turned out to be a long time, to treat it almost as if it had happened to someone else. Perhaps if I had attempted it as a memoir, a sense of catharsis may have been plausible. But I was not interested in writing memoir. Memoir is 'what happened', whereas fiction is 'what could or might have happened', allowing adventures beyond the stifling parameters of what has

already been witnessed or felt. I was hoping to find the richness
of a place where memory, yearning, speculation and melodrama
could meet and concoct what felt most true, and most thrilling.
'What makes it fiction is the nature of the imaginative act,' Toni
Morrison said in her own take on autobiography and memoir.[8]
Possibly on one level, the excitement of this imaginative act was
what may have been cathartic, the idea that a creative magic
could be culled from devastation.

I spent two years after that initial conception on the sofa
trying and failing to write *26a*. One of the big problems was that
I didn't know how to write a novel. I had no idea how to construct or arrange long-form narrative. I drew up a plan,
horizontally across the page, the rationale for this being that we
read horizontally and I wanted to see it laid out in the same way.
This was useful in that it enabled me to attempt to write scenes
in some form of onward order, but they did not amount to an
effective whole. Another big problem was that the story I was
trying to tell was a not yet a story in my head – it was a happening, and the happening itself, the death, was still caught in a
shock of time. I was still stunned by it, the fact of it, and I was
writing from the happening outwards, thus beginning the novel
with the death and then moving backwards and forwards in
time, so that the reader, my perception of whom at that point
was negligible, was denied the opportunity to experience the
same shock, and therefore the magic resulting from the shock.
What I needed was some major distance between the site of loss
and the story of loss, if not in time, then at least in geography,
which was where the extraction from London was crucial: it
enabled me to imagine the world of the story from afar.

There was one final significant problem I had been having,
relating to the above and also corresponding with another of the
questions I am often asked: Is your writing autobiographical?
This is a question asked more often, I believe, and with more

accusatory weight, of women than of men, and it bears a faint insinuation of craft deficiency, a suggestion that the autobiographical nature of a story lowers its social relevance. There is a line in a Carmen Maria Machado story that perfectly captures this: 'Men are permitted to write concealed autobiography, but I cannot do the same?'[9] I was frankly terrified of the exposure involved in telling the story I wanted to tell, and the only bravery I had mustered so far was fuelled by an absolute faith that it had a social and spiritual value. Really, though, I did not want to be a public lone twin. I did not want to be compared in real life to the people in my story. I did not want to be pitied. I did not even especially want to write about depression and suicide. And so all in all I had not yet managed to achieve the level of extra bravery required to fly fully in the face of the traditional, dismissive patriarchal reception of female subjectivity, where so much that is valuable and meaningful lies. In order to do that, I would need to pull away the internalised gossamer of such belittlements and write fearlessly, guiltlessly, from the ferocity of the bruised self. This is where reading Jean Rhys helped.

In 1914, after her heart was broken, Jean Rhys became a writer. As she recalls in her autobiography, *Smile Please*, it was an entirely instinctive thing. She'd moved into a room in Fulham that had a 'bare and very ugly table', and she'd brightened it with some coloured quill pens and exercise books. Then, 'after supper that night . . . it happened. My fingers tingled, and the palms of my hands.' She sat down and filled three and a half exercise books with writing, which later became the foundation for her third novel, *Voyage in the Dark*. Her other novels are no less lacking in melancholia and malaise, generally drawn from her own life, yet without gush or sentiment, instead they are wrought with a hard, dry wit and fierce intelligence. Rhys made an art out of the articulation of sadness in its many forms, from despondency to insanity, and the outlook of the work was not a limited or claustrophobic one, entangled as it was with the impact of class, migration, colonialism and male dominance on subjective experience and identity. Her writing is as visceral and self-absorbed as it is kaleidoscopic and socially representative.

Initial responses to Rhys's work in the 1920s and 1930s commended her precise, experimental style (drawing parallels with Katherine Mansfield and Ernest Hemingway), but there was disappointment from critics at what was felt to be a dearth of worthwhile thematic content. 'It is a waste of talent,' complained *The Times Literary Supplement*. The dark days of lonely, drunken, wandering women – in some sense always the same woman – her pained interactions and stark observations, were not seen as noteworthy by a literary establishment that typically posited the male voice as public decree and the female voice as more limited or domestic in scope. Beyond the aftermath of the First World War, a proliferation of war memoirs turned autobiographical writing into something of a modernist vogue, celebrating contributions by male writers like Cecil Day-Lewis, Graham Greene and Stephen Spender, but similar novelistic or confessional texts by Rhys, Dorothy Richardson, Stevie Smith and Elizabeth Bowen tended to be met with less gravitas, despite their formal and stylistic innovation. It was not until 1966, after years in obscurity, that Jean Rhys became widely acknowledged as a literary heavyweight.

Born and raised on the Caribbean island of Dominica, Rhys moved to England at the age of seventeen and stayed for ten years, working as a chorus girl, artists' model, and then living off an allowance from her ex-lover. She escaped to Paris with her first husband, where she met the writer Ford Maddox Ford who read and encouraged her work. A collection of stories, *The Left Bank*, was published in 1927, after which she returned to London and published four novels, *Quartet, After Leaving*

Mr Mackenzie (my favourite), *Voyage in the Dark* and *Good Morning, Midnight* (my second favourite). Her work did not sell well and, although *Good Morning, Midnight*, in which she perfected her rootless, brittle, self-effacing stock heroine, received good critical feedback, it fell into the cracks of World War II and her books subsequently went out of print. A 1950s BBC radio dramatisation of *Midnight* sparked new interest in Rhys's writing, bringing her to resume work on a novel she'd started years before, an adaptation of Jane Eyre. *Wide Sargasso Sea* was published in 1966 and was an award-winning comeback, spawning three more publications before and shortly after her death, the stories *Tigers Are Better-Looking* (mostly written in the 1940s) and *Sleep It Off Lady*, and the unfinished, posthumously published autobiography. By the end of her career, Rhys had been dubbed by the writer Al Alvarez in the *New York Times* 'the best living novelist' – but the acclaim had come too late.

'Oh Peggy,' she wrote to a friend in 1941, 'I can't bear much more of my hideous life. It revolts me quite simply.'[10] She hated cold, grey, brutal England. She was 'smashed' twice by the deaths of her second and third husbands. Loneliness and isolation had shrouded her since childhood, when she had begun to immerse herself in books. Although she had never especially wanted to write – 'I wished to be happy and peaceful and obscure. I was *dragged* into writing by a series of coincidences' – she nevertheless viewed it as the only thing that justified her existence as a human being: 'If I stop writing,' she wrote in *Smile Please*, 'my life will have been an abject failure . . . I will not have earned death.'[11] Rhys's experience of the bohemian circus of 1920s Paris, which might have provided some sense of community, was less convivial and glamorous than that of some of her contemporaries such as Djuna Barnes or Nancy Cunard; she is described (by Shari Benstock in *Women of the Left Bank*) as someone 'moving like a ghost among the expatriates'.

Unlike many of her wealthy peers who lived off inheritances and allowances, she slept in cheap hotels and had to scrape together enough to survive. She was painfully shy and went for long walks alone, as does her character Julia Martin in *After Leaving Mr Mackenzie*, 'so anxious not to meet anybody that she always kept to the backstreets as much as possible'.

It is difficult to think of Rhys's work without thinking of her life. The stories of *The Left Bank* were based on her experiences in Paris; *Voyage in the Dark* fictionalised her time as a chorus girl and the love affair that brought her to the page; *Quartet* was drawn from her first marriage; in *Good Morning, Midnight* there is reference to the death of her son. Her childhood in Dominica resurfaces again and again in her work as landscapes, dreams, nostalgia, most palpably in *Wide Sargasso Sea*. 'I can't make things up,' Rhys once professed. 'I can't invent . . . I just write about what happened. Not that my books are entirely my life – but almost.'[12] The psychological enunciation in her writing is often so pristine that it is hard to imagine that it was not at some point actually *felt* by the writer herself. This is Julia, in *After Leaving Mr Mackenzie*:

> She walked on through the fog into Tottenham Court Road. The houses and the people passing were withdrawn, nebulous. There was only a grey fog shot with yellow lights, and the cold breath on her face, and the ghost of herself coming out of the fog to meet her.
>
> The ghost was thin and eager. It wore a long, very tight check shirt, a short dark-blue coat, and a bunch of violets bought from the old man in Woburn Square. It drifted up to her and passed her in the fog. And she had the feeling that, like the old man, it looked at her coldly, without recognising her.

An example of a character alienated both internally and externally. Rhys's protagonists are the lost ones, women living uncertain, broken lives, though they are at the same time fiercely individualistic, despising of the monotony of conformity and convention, like Rhys herself, who in a letter to Francis Wyndham in 1964 dubbed herself a 'savage individualist'.[13] Anna, the protagonist of *Voyage in the Dark*, observing a woman lodging in the same boarding house as her, writes, 'She looked just like most other people, which is a big advantage. An ant, just like all the other ants.' In Rhys's fiction the 'belongers' are the same as insects, objects, prisoners, yet her heroines cannot help but envy them the relative ease implied by their surrender to the societal machine. In the hallway of Anna's boarding house, there is a table and on top of it a plant, 'made of rubber with shiny, bright red leaves, five-pointed'. Anna reacts to the plant with an absurd jealousy and a simultaneous, underlying recognition of its imprisonment: 'I couldn't take my eyes off it. It looked proud of itself, as if it knew that it fitted in with the house and the street and the spiked iron railings outside.'

One of the things I appreciated most about Rhys's work while devouring it in my student room in Norwich was her technique of projecting the emotional states of her characters outside of their minds, onto the external world. The rooms they inhabit, the streets they walk, the people they come across, have a piercing, warped physicality that conveys, either by reflection or by contrast, the characters' depressed and terrified inner spaces. Julia's landlady at her 'sixteen francs a night' Paris hotel has 'red eyelids'. The room she is renting is gloomy, with a 'one-eyed aspect because the solitary window was very much to one side'. Fireplaces are cold instead of warm, houses are not safe but menacing, symbols of eternal, ubiquitous betrayal. Julia feels better when she is 'locked in her room', and when she finds herself somewhere physically beautiful she feels utterly, even offensively, out of place: 'when she looked around the room it seemed to her a very beautiful room, and she felt that she had no right to sit there and intrude her sordid wish somehow to keep alive into that beautiful room'. Rhys puts her women in ordinary places in extreme states of mind, and thereby creates a world brought to life by the charisma of despair. 'The real subject of autobiography is not one's experience but one's consciousness,' wrote Patricia Hampl of memoir writing, which seems relevant here. 'And to reveal one's consciousness is more intimate – and eternal – than to reveal one's experience,' as consciousness touches 'everything in existence'.[14]

When working on a novel, it is not uncommon for a writer to feel that they are engaged in a kind of sorcery, that an uncanny, extra-dimensional force is aiding your work. Hilary Mantel described once that the right books will 'appear in your hand'[15] while in a library, and Toni Morrison has described that she witnessed her character Beloved rising out of the Hudson River towards her. Becoming acquainted with Jean Rhys's oeuvre while searching for a new way in to the writing of *26a* seemed similarly auspicious. Through the frank, uncompromising honesty in her work, her determination to convey life as she saw it, harvesting her experiences in order to offer something to literature that was true and exact, and in doing so with such careful, cool artistry, she helped me find a voice with which to craft my story. I was buoyed by her steely sadness, her fine articulation of the manifestations of depression, and I saw how it was possible to achieve an authorial distance caught somewhere between empathy and ruthlessness. Above all, through a combination of reading, writing and literary conversation both on and off the page, I arrived at a place where I could put aside my fears and reservations about the source material for my novel and concentrate on what I urgently wanted to show to the world. What did I want to explore or contribute? What was its social value? What was the essential resonance I wanted to leave behind? These were the important questions, and my job as a writer was to find a way to answer them.

It was not easy, those nine monastic months spent in that room with my back to the window as I wrote another draft. I would go for crying fifteen-minute walks around the neigh-bourhood on my break times. I made intricate feta and pine-nut salads for lunch and ate them alone in the kitchen so as not to interrupt my zone with another human voice. Three mornings a week I swam in the campus pool. At the end of the writing day I read for ninety minutes, after beginning the writing day with fifteen minutes of poetry. The clock and the routine were fun-damental; they meant that the heights and plummets of creative activity were safely reined while invited to thrive by the freeing commitment of regularity. It was hard sitting there with my back to the sun and the sacrifice was real, but it is the best way I have found to produce a novel. Three-quarters of the way through, one evening, I found a dead cockroach on my carpet, lying on its back. I am very, very frightened of cockroaches and was alarmed. It was a sign, though, that the novel was alive and bristling, its emotions and internal imagery, like those of Rhys's women, projecting onto the external world.

Writing facilitates immortality, an enduring voice, conjures magic. I often think of Oscar Allen and his volcano, his desire to bring new forms to the surface of the earth. This seems the innate calling of artistic work, and within it, we might hope to be of some benefit to others. A few years after *26a* was finished, once the book was published and had been read widely enough to draw an audience to a university auditorium, a man came up to the signing table, where I signed his book and gave it back to him. He told me that he had read *26a* when he was going through a depression, and that it had made him feel understood. It was a small moment of rightness, of unassumed validation, with a power at times to anchor me in the vastness of this journey.

© Diana Evans, 2024

The Five Psychological Stages of Novel Writing

1. Doubt

You believe it cannot be done. You believe it must be done. But you are the only person who can do it. You cannot do it. You must do it. So begins the tussle, which will go on for possibly years in one form or another, with increasing intensity, until you get to near the end of Stage Five. This conflicted outset is the assemblage of fear and faith, an uncomfortable, unsettling union. They run in opposite directions, one dark, one bright; one telling you it is hopeless and it's best you give up and do something better with your time, the other professing your great responsibility to this very important work. Logistically speaking, Stage One is the phase of argument and persuasion. It's all speculation. Nothing is actually achieved apart from maybe some uncertain note-making – you might even try writing a scene here and there to test out the idea, to see if it will float (usually it doesn't because it doesn't yet attach to anything – a novel is a cluster of attachments, a pattern). You are trying to convince yourself. You will go to a library and browse the shelves, select a few disparate books and take them with you to a quiet table to see if they hold any positive signs, any magical message or enigma that yes, this is what you must write, now. You will go to a museum and feel the command of history in the wings of your yearning. You stare at cold, random objects.

You are quite lost. No one can help you, except for one or two chosen ones. You will put too much onus on the things they say, their responses and surprises. They will disappoint and elate you without understanding why. You cannot stay here forever. Your existence is becoming impossible.

2. Preparing

Finally, you have accepted that some onward motion needed to take place. You have made a commitment. You are going to give yourself to the task of producing this impossible thing that only you can produce. This is definitely a better place, though no less frightening. At least now the searching, the exploring, is clearly focused on the intended reality of the thing; an existential swamp has been surpassed, conquered. If its murky creatures remain, laughing from the sidelines, you will walk on by, absorbed in your duties. These include making lists – of characters, events, objects, moments of dialogue, descriptions and small details. You go for long walks with the people in your story and imagine the world from their angle. You will take more constructive trips to the library and when you find yourself reading along blind alleys you will change tack, repointing yourself in the right direction. It is about following energy, trusting instinct. Instinct is all a writer has with which to spiritually survive. At some stage in this stage, your research will feel detrimental or superfluous. You will feel that you are losing an original thread and no longer want to hear other voices except in their echoes. Again, you are aware of your complete isolation, and its crucialness. You will spend a day or two pacing the carpet of your room with pieces of paper strewn across the floor – your notes, lists, Post-its and snippets of scenes. In a leaning towards order, you will remember what Hilary Mantel said about resisting the urge to organise your material so as to maintain a sense of looseness.[16] You may nevertheless make a plan – horizontally, the way books are read – which will prove at some juncture useless, yet will steady you at the precipice to the fathomless ocean of writing.

3. Writing

Here at last. In the wide unbridled swimming. This is the freedom time. This is where anything can happen and you are allowed to make as much mess as you want – throw paint at the wall, throw your characters off cliffs, off the edges of the Earth, have them say outrageous nonsensical things to one other. If you exploit this freedom enough they will talk to you, often, or more precisely you will hear them talking to each other. You will hear their voices in your head while you are listening to the radio or walking in the woods or buying butterhead salad. You will find them much more interesting than your own family, and you will find yourself exiting a room or a conversation in order to write down what they have just said. For there are essential clues here. Nothing can be missed. You must be at attention at all times, even in the middle of the night, even while dreaming, when a piece of dialogue or a clue might permeate sleep, forcing you to switch on a lamp and reach for your notebook. This is your favourite, most liveable stage. Your whole self goes into it; you can feel yourself being poured in. You are insanely, brilliantly alive. It is like summer, the world looks brighter, the outlines of trees, landscapes and vistas are clearer. It is not a good idea to go on holiday or undertake any major shift in location during this stage (unless it is to work), because the uncomfortable reality of it is that you are incapable of experiencing contentment anywhere else but in front of the novel, sitting before it, at the coalface, alone at your desk, with the rest of the world going on outside. Your exhilaration is private and untranslatable. Nobody understands your shiny secret happiness. They only witness the tortured one who has been dragged away from her work to be sociable, who does not return phone calls because speaking might be dangerous.

4. Revision

But does it make any sense? Has that period of exhilarating freedom amounted to anything coherent? Do you have 'a novel'? The answer is no, which is why this stage is the hardest of all – you now have to make it make sense. You have to make everything connect and the pattern work. Uncertainty returns, deeper than before. You are required to read the reams of nonsense you have written and make agonising decisions about what will stay and what must go. This is the time of the losing of the darlings, which has never been your strong point. They are scattered all over the floor with their beautiful curlicues and flourishes, along with some scenes that don't belong, a character or two who is no longer needed. The overall structural imperative looms heavily in your way, and solidifying it is the most difficult task, the one whose avenue usually does not become clear until near the end of the journey. You are thinking about the project in macro terms, hacking through woods to reach the clearing: as the saying goes, you cannot see the wood for the trees. Immense bravery, it takes, to make it through this stage, as well as persistence. You might be labouring for years and you may feel that you will never get out, that there is no end to it, no completion, that all this work might eventually come to nothing, and it will seem that any other potential project you have ever thought about writing is what you should be doing instead of this, this timewasting. Leave it, the inner voice might say, the world will continue just as well without it. Yet that vital nugget of original faith keeps you going, the part of you that believes it must be done, that the book must exist and the world could be better for it. You have such grand illusions of the social importance of the work that they have the power to lift you up when you are an exhausted bleeding wreck on the forest floor.

5. Completion

If you survived that last bit, Stage Four, now you are on the home straight. Jubilation is possible, in theory. The structure is in place, the pattern has revealed itself and every element of the novel is sufficiently justified. You have realised that the plot is not what it's about but a device on which to hang the scenes about what it is really about, which is a load off your mind. This stage is by far the easiest. What you are trying to produce already exists, and all you have to do is make it sing, massage it, bring every sentence to an optimum state. It is this close, delicious, fine-tuning work that will keep you wrapped in the quietude of your study for hours on end, even through long nights until you hear the voices of the early birds rising with the new day. You can still hear your characters talking to each other, and they will bring ever new, ever more specific things to the table as a result of your commitment. It is a living, breathing thing, this creature you have created, and it is not finished forming until the last sentence. The ending is important, of course, perhaps the most weighted, sacred moment. Everything must fall right. It must be the right beat, the right resonance, the right accumulation of meaning and sensation. Endings make you nervous, that it might not go right, that the directions you have taken might not be capable of leading you to the right places. Afterwards, though, you are filled with warm achievement and huge relief. You look at it one last time and then leave, get as far away from it as you can, for long enough to return to it with new eyes, like a stranger.

WritersMosaic, 2022

Updike and Time's Up

'Rabbits and treacle are just not my scene.' So said a fellow writer to me recently when asked her opinion of John Updike. 'I can't get along with him,' she said with a huff of exasperation, 'it's like going through treacle.' The richness of his language being her main objection, there are of course more serious complaints, the pinnacle of which is probably the jibe once related by David Foster Wallace in a 1997 *Observer* book review, 'just a penis with a thesaurus'. And that was over twenty years ago. Now it's worse. A fortnight ago the literary critic and novelist James Wood dismissed Updike as 'unreadable' on account of his misogyny. Maybe even worse than that, another fellow writer whose opinion I asked, this time a man, answered, 'Who?'

John Updike has fallen from grace. As far as feminism is concerned, he was never in the vicinity of grace in the first place, what with his degrading and debasing portrayals of women and his helpless centralising of the (his) libidinous male ego. Artistically, though, his greatness has always been irrefutable, to those who like treacle at least. A longstanding darling of *The New Yorker*, he published reams of exquisite short stories capturing, like birds in flight, like living, breathing things, the most prosaic yet sensuous details of ordinary life. Poems too, and essays, and reviews — words flowed from him at a steady rate of a thousand a day, filling around sixty books, most famously the Harry 'Rabbit' Angstrom tetralogy which Julian Barnes in 2009 described as 'still the greatest postwar American novel',[17] twenty years after his first summation, and which won Updike two Pulitzers.

But things are different now. In this time of #MeToo and Time's Up and paedophiliac gymnastics coaches and harassment-shamed MPs and unbridled Hollywood penises and depraved charity workers and whatever's coming up next week, our heroes are being questioned. The anxiety is real. It's got so bad I worry about my daughter's hockey changing rooms and what random pervert may lurk in wait. A harmless-looking man holds a lift door open for me at a station and I'm wondering at his inner psychopath and opportunist pussy-grabber and whether I am going to be the one to meet his next irrepressible impulse. Appearing before us is the historic and enduring reality of a widespread lack of male control over the male corpus, making it a pretty strange time to be appreciative of the lofty creative fruits of male narcissism.

Yet, on the corner of my desk, from the cover of *The Early Stories*, Updike's face looks softly out into an unknown middle distance, waiting to be read. On my bedside table among a pile of other books (Mary Gaitskill, James Baldwin, William Burroughs [yikes!], Virginia Woolf), he is walking along a beach in a white shirt on the cover of his biography, looking windswept and satisfied. Me, I like the treacle. I really like the treacle. John Updike's sentences are like hot-air balloons drifting through a dazzling harlequin sky. They are life-affirming. They are, in fact, narcissistic, but in a good way, which is that they are interested in the achievement of their own beauty, aware as they are of the responsibility of this beauty: of Updike's overarching desire to 'give the mundane its beautiful due.'[18] Influenced throughout his literary career by an inclination towards drawing and painting (he spent a year at the Ruskin School of Art in Oxford before becoming a writer), he approached the page as canvas, his lens rich and encyclopaedically precise, his clauses bearing the texture and specificity of carefully considered brushstrokes. How can we (at least I) not be made momentarily happier by a sentence such as 'Invisible rivulets running brokenly make the low land of the estate sing', from the garden scene in *Rabbit, Run*. Or, from *Couples*, a novel in which it is admittedly harder to find wonderful sentences that are not encased by mentions of breasts, but still: 'Shed needles from the larches had collected in streaks and puddles on the tarpaper and formed rusty ochre drifts along the wooden balustrade and the grooved aluminium base of the sliding glass doors'. This is profound sensitivity to nature and domestic realism merging seamlessly in a mastery of rhythmic description. He does occasionally go too far — when is it necessary to describe a toothbrush as 'an acolyte of matinal devotion', from the short story 'Dentistry and Doubt'?[19] — but this by the sweet-toothed can be forgiven.

Virginia Woolf said in *A Room of One's Own* that books have a way of influencing each other, and it is certainly true that Updike's *Couples* was a prime impetus behind my novel *Ordinary People*. I remember clearly the moment that I read the opening page, in which Piet and Angela Hanema are in their bedroom changing after a party. I was in my own bedroom, in the late afternoon, which I also shared with a man in the usual and really quite oppressive marital tradition, and I could picture vividly the Hanemas' 'low-ceilinged colonial' chamber whose woodwork was painted 'the shade of off-white commercially called eggshell', and the 'spring midnight' pressing in on the 'cold windows'. Somehow the woodwork, the windows, combined with the 'reddened fingertips' of Angela's hands, Piet's red hair, made them seem so acutely human, so manifest, so *visible*. And it struck me, with a hint of anger, when was the last time I had seen a black man or a black woman doing something in a book that did not have anything specific and/or tragic to do with racism, migration, slavery, poverty, injustice, knife crime or exotic food? How often do middle-class black people in books get to just live in their damn houses and open and close their wardrobes and be aware of each other's fingertips? I desired visibility on a most basic level. It seemed incredibly important, all of a sudden, for the purposes of the humanisation and normalisation of what Lauryn Hill might phrase 'my men and my women', that some brown person in a novel should be witnessed experiencing an ordinary domestic irritation such as Rabbit's problem with his coat hanger not being accessible enough for him to hang up his coat neatly when he gets home from work; and in the careful, specific rendering of such an irritation are embedded the modern manifestations and legacies of what black people have experienced throughout the history that has left us invisible as whole and sentient beings.

I am grateful to Updike for that moment. I am grateful also to Richard Yates for *Revolutionary Road* and James Salter for *Light Years*, novels that likewise posit the domestic realm as a valid site for literature (if 'Great Male Narcissists' come in threes – Wallace aligned Updike with Philip Roth and Norman Mailer[20] – these were mine). As for female writers, I could not have done without the work of Jean Rhys, Doris Lessing, Jhumpa Lahiri and Rachel Cusk in finding the courage to write about what are typically and disparagingly considered 'feminine' themes: when a woman writes about marriage, she is writing about a marriage; when a man writes about marriage, he is writing about Society, which in the case of Updike is interesting because he seemed so incapable of seeing clearly beyond his own viewpoint. Angela Hanema is sentient only through Piet's randy, disappointed eyes, his preoccupation with his diminishing quota of life's sex. What is missing from much of Updike's work is a convincing female consciousness. In *Couples*, women are frequently described in animalistic, inanimate or juvenile terms. Angela is 'a fair soft brown-haired woman, thirty-four, going heavy in the haunches and waist yet with a girl's fine hard ankles'. Georgene, with whom Piet is having an affair at the start of the novel, has 'a strangely prominent coccyx', 'the good start of a tail', and is 'more bone than Angela'. And how could any feminist or indeed any woman not be offended by a sentence like, 'As she struggled, lamplight struck zigzag fire from her slip and static electricity made its nylon adhere to her flank'? Her *flank*? Never mind the fancy fire and the nylon and the giving of the beautiful due to the mundane, don't horses have flanks? In Piet's world – that is, his mind, which within the system of patriarchy is the world as well – women are at once childlike and bestial, intellectually shaded yet viscerally more potent, arousing the male urge to simultaneously conquer and be mothered.

It's hard for a female reader to go along with this and feel nurtured or recognised in her reading experience. The thing is, though, Piet and Rabbit are ridiculous. They're big, salivating, calamitous boys playing out the lost fantasies of youth in the bodies of faltering men. They're sad, and I think on some level Updike knows this, the inadequacy of men, their weakness in the face of their given power. Or maybe I'm giving him too much credit. 'My duty as a writer is to make the best record I can of life as I understand it,' he once said, 'and that duty takes precedence for me over all these other considerations.'[21] It's so easy for men to say things like that and get away with it, to stand firmly on the solid ground of their obliviousness. But he kept to his duty, which is less easy for the artist to do. Oblivious to his myopia, he painted his wordy pictures. Are we to discard him because he got so much wrong? Should we take the pictures down? Burn the books? Turn off the music? Leave all the sexists lying by the side of the road clutching their art while we walk on towards cultural purity? Am I not allowed to have treacle anymore because of Donald Trump? Not forgetting, it must be noted, that this particular treacle does contain quite eyewatering levels of racism reminiscent of Donald Trump, which I must say

I find harder to sidestep, but the point is, if all the offensive, morally debased and denigrating matter was omitted from the widely peopled canvas of the imagination, what would be left, and would it be enough, would it be real, what would we miss?

The other day I was in my kitchen with my feminist older sister, a silver-dreadlocked mixed-race woman of vegan diet and staunch politics, and I decided to show her the video to Kendrick Lamar's 'Humble' because I had just seen him in concert and was still high. I knew straight away it was a mistake. We wear our feminism differently. My feminism runs so deep that I have always felt reluctant to name it as if it were something extra to myself. It is an assertion of my feminism that I do not see why I should be deprived of the world's dopest beats just because the lyrics or the images do not please my feminism (within reason – William Burroughs's shooting of his wife and then hardly even acknowledging her as a human being kind of spoiled *Junky* for me). Anyway, my sister was offended by the video's bare cleavages and waving buttocks. Lamar was myopic to think that women might appreciate real stretch-marked buttocks over the usual unattainable airbrushed ones. Better no buttocks at all, or at least male ones as well, for balance? There is still a long way to go. My sister's mouth pursed in distaste. I could sense her disappointment in me. I was no longer nodding to the beats, but continuing to enjoy them in secret.

Dorothy West, *The Wedding* et al.

'Little sister' to Zora Neale Hurston. 'The Kid' and would-be wife to Langston Hughes, if he had said yes. Rediscovered at eighty-five by Jacqueline Onassis. Adapted by Oprah starring Halle Berry. Dorothy West, by her own description, was the 'best-known unknown writer of the time'[22] – the time being, ostensibly, the Harlem Renaissance, though her first novel was not published until 1948, her second almost fifty years later. But Harlem was where it all began: that sizzling, surging artistic retaliation of the 1920s, of which West, fresh from the black elite of Boston, found herself a part. She was one of its youngest members, and at the time of her death in 1998 the last one standing. Her career is a rare, enigmatic mélange of obscurity, revival and longevity.

Hurston and West were roommates for a while after sharing second place in a short-story competition run by the journal of civil-rights organisation the National Urban League, which was what first brought West to New York. Following a year in Russia with him in 1932, she did ask Hughes to marry her, in writing, though they subsequently drifted in different directions, marriage becoming instead an object of dark scrutiny and dispensable complexity in West's fiction. Subversions of convention were more to her palette, and this bohemian whirl of writers and artists gathering around 125th Street and beyond proved both nurturing and irresistible; there was also the poet Countee Cullen, novelist and poet Claude McKay, writer and editor Wallace Thurman, in whose loft apartment she would often be found, sitting on the floor.

While most of her comrades were writing about African American lives of the working classes, West's was a thoroughly middle-class milieu, drawn from the realities and observations of her privileged background as the only child of one of Boston's richest black families. She wrote 'posh black' at a time when 'broke black' was in vogue, and this sits at the heart of her flickering obscurity, a shortsightedness in mainstream culture that struggled to perceive blackness as anything more than one-dimensional. There was no room for nuance in the story of the great racial oppression. This was no place for chauffeurs and piano lessons and private tutors and maids and first-world problems and 'lawn croquet and lemonade', as featured in West's second novel *The Wedding*, a bestseller on its publication in 1995 and swiftly televised by Oprah Winfrey's Harpo Productions. Convinced into apathy by the notion that there was no appetite for the subtler, inner politics of the black bourgeois, it had taken Jacqueline Onassis – then a Doubleday editor and neighbour of West at her home in affluent Martha's Vineyard – to persuade her otherwise and coax her back to work on the novel, the precursor to which had been originally rejected by her publisher on the belief that it wouldn't sell. Her first novel, *The Living Is Easy*, although critically acclaimed, had not been a commercial success, and this was taken as fair indication that the reading public had no interest in 'black writing' that did not mirror their limited understanding of 'black experience'.

West did not see herself as a political writer. She hated the Black Panthers and the drastic divisive doctrine of pre-Mecca Malcolm X. She did not march or 'do' civil rights, yet her work is deeply concerned with the insidious and warped permeations of race into everyday lives. *The Wedding*, set in Martha's Vineyard in the 1950s, is about colourism; it's about the profound psychological impasse posed by slavery and colonialism that envisioned black deliverance in the emulation of whiteness.

Gram, the elderly matriarch of the story, a Southern belle raised on a plantation, is heartbroken when her daughter marries a black man, crossing 'her true white blood, her blue blood, with colored'. She wants nothing whatsoever to get in the way of her great-granddaughter Shelby's planned wedding to a white jazz musician, thereby freeing her in her last days from the 'burden of living colored'. Shelby's father, though, having dutifully married a light-skinned woman of his own Ivy League class and lost out on real love, can only see a similar calculating in his daughter, accusing her (himself) of lacking the courage to follow her heart. All of them are confused, even eventually Shelby herself, so entangled are they in a claustrophobia of race and class that they cannot tell which feelings are their own and which other people's, or society's, the distinction itself tragically fading away the older they get.

The people with any sense are children, West implies, the possibilities they create within us to transcend these demarcations, if we can only keep from dragging our young along with us, which we nevertheless must. When Shelby as a child goes missing one day in the neighbourhood, the people looking for her cannot find her because they are looking for what they think of as a black child, rather than a 'blond-haired, blue-eyed child' possessing the 'protective coloring' of the Coles family. When Shelby is eventually found, Gram is faced with her question, 'Am I colored?' 'Yes,' Gram has no choice but to answer, and Shelby is relieved, 'not because she was black, but because she was something definite'. The effort to shield her from race, or overlook it, had proved to be counterproductive, even dangerous, deeming Shelby's beautiful innocence useless in practical terms. West's point is not that colour doesn't matter, but that it shouldn't. Children also must 'learn race', though in a way that equips them for it, that allows them to walk strongly through the world. 'It's a private and internal struggle,' Shelby's sister

Liz says, speaking of the fierce love she feels for her own child, born a clear, unprotected brown. 'And to win she will have to fight back without bitterness, not replacing her hurt with hate but letting that hurt enrich her experience.'

As well as providing important insights into the emergence of the African American middle class – the waiters and porters saving their tips and sending their sons to high school, the starting of small businesses, the gradual generational learning of a new 'style of living' involving summer residences and wearing silk – West's work illuminates further subtleties that broaden our understanding of slavery's bitter legacy and the American social strata. She writes of the difference between the showy black New Yorkers and the more reserved Bostonians who are not quite ready to flaunt their diamonds. She tells of the 'Southern aristocrat's uncompromising contempt for poor whites', and also of the ironic yearning of many blacks who'd travelled north, freed from the possibilities of lynching and the Klan, for the 'indescribable beauty of the South [that] would haunt them forever', and 'make the babbling old beg to go home and die'.[23] West's father, Isaac West, was born into slavery. He was seven years old when it ended, and later travelled north from Virginia to become a wealthy grocer, an example of triumph over circumstance that West writes movingly of in her essay 'The Gift'. Her mother, Rachel West, was the daughter of emancipated slaves from South Carolina, a charming dynamo of a woman who insisted on good breeding and good behaviour for her daughter. Such close familial connections to the horrors of the trade render West's voice both inherently political and deeply empathetic, able to address with equal conviction the trauma of captivity and the peaks and pitfalls of freedom.

West began writing stories at the age of seven, and was first published at fourteen, in *The Boston Post*. She was still only seventeen when she tied with the already established Hurston with her story 'The Typewriter', which opens *The Richer, The Poorer*, her collected essays and short fiction covering the period between 1926 and 1987. A graduate of Boston University and the Columbia University School of Journalism, she toyed with acting for a while with a bit part in the original stage production of *Porgy and Bess*, and when the whirl of the Harlem Renaissance was over founded a quarterly literary magazine, *Challenge*, to try and revive it. This failed, was revisited briefly in 1937 with co-editor Richard Wright (whom she 'was never crazy about . . . because he was so timid and afraid of white people'[24]), and she subsequently worked as a welfare investigator in Harlem as the Great Depression deepened. This provided material for several of her stories, capturing poor blacks in moments of fleeting fortune to highlight their plight, such as the boy given a penny by his father in 'The Penny', and the married couple thrown into welfare anxiety by a gambling win in 'Jack In The Pot'. In 1940 West began writing two short stories a month for *The New York Daily News*, the first black author to do so, and continued these commissions until 1960. She left New York in 1943 to settle permanently in Martha's Vineyard, and there contributed columns to *The Vineyard Gazette*. She neither married nor mothered, but cared for relatives while working on her writing.

The longevity of West's fiction lies in its relevance to both historical and modern concerns, its consistent acknowledgement that modernity is the unfortunate manifestation of history. Her themes are both intimate and universal: her exploration of the murky innards of marriage in stories like 'The Envelope' and 'Fluff and Mr Ripley', of the unsettling mysteries of death in 'Funeral', the anguish of a black parent who wishes their child personal freedom but bows instead to the burden of race in 'An Unimportant Man'. She is a writer of huge compassion and acute observation and, simultaneously, of dazzling style. There is a mystery to her sentences, a creeping idiosyncrasy, a lush and dreamy boldness. She does not shy from the full dramatic potential of a death scene or a love scene, but reaches instead, like the best writers, for the almost unimaginable, the weird and the unexpected. A woman gets out of bed one morning feeling cold, and the cold slowly becomes death, and West tells us, in this scene from *The Wedding*, 'Out of the intensity of her physical oneness had come a mystical communication in which she had taken his dying into the warm bed of her body, not to die with him, not to die for her, but to fight for his life with the supernatural strength the resisting flesh stores for the hour before eternity.' Her tone is loosely biblical and alluring, attesting a deep humanity to her characters while luxuriating in the power of description and the beauty of language. Her poetics abound, a man with a voice like 'a cello, a flute, a clap of thunder', a phantom woman who 'drifted out of his arms'.[25]

It is most often women whose voices are lost in the marching canons of literature and its movements, and it is more often black women. Dorothy West's contributions to the documentation of her world may have been routinely suppressed and misunderstood by the tunnel vision of mainstream culture, but her work is more relevant than ever. There must be room for nuance, for subtlety, it reminds us, for the myriad distinctions among people and communities. By showing the whole of something you show the whole truth, the true picture, not just one part of it, and we understand more widely, feel more generously, connect more powerfully, with greater wealth of spirit. 'Color was a false distinction; love was not,' she wrote,[26] and that is a message that will continue to resound.

Foreword to *The Wedding* by Dorothy West,
Virago, 2019; *Guardian*, 2019

Scary Houses: Reading Richard Yates

Among the bits of paper stuck on the wall by my desk is this quote about the life of Richard Yates: 'But still the writing went on, every day, like some terrible prison sentence – a sentence to write sentences. The writing . . . is what kept Yates alive far longer than his body deserved. The writing was the life force, with which the poor ordinary life could not keep up. By his early forties Yates seemed much older than his years and coughed and wheezed continuously. He did not drink during the day – while he was writing – but often drank himself senseless at night.'

The quote is from a *Guardian* review of Blake Bailey's biography of Yates, *A Tragic Honesty,*[27] and simply a glance in its direction can galvanise a lacklustre writing day in the direction of productivity. It seems to contain an essential realism about the level of commitment and personal sacrifice required of a serious writer of fiction. You are governed and consumed by it. Your love for it is the keeper of the key to your prison, and while you are imprisoned you are blissfully free. Almost nothing (only the well-being of your children) is more important than turning up and continuing to write. When the world turns away from you with disinterest or discontent, you carry on regardless, because to write is to live and to not write is fatal.

The world turned away repeatedly from Richard Yates, who produced seven novels and two collections of short stories (only one of his stories was ever published in the holy vessel of *The New Yorker*, eight years after his death). His prose is neither highly intellectual nor highly stylised, two of the traits that might have classified him as 'a writer's writer' in attempting to explain his recurrent obscurity in his lifetime. Instead, his work is characterised by an accessible, brutally clear, strident and unfussy mode of address, depicting the mundane yet agonised existences of ordinary American men and women in the decades following the mid-point of the twentieth century. The most well-known of his novels is the 1961 National Book Award-nominated *Revolutionary Road*, about the suburban marital turmoil of Frank and April Wheeler, played by Leonardo Di Caprio and Kate Winslet in the 2008 film adaptation which bolstered a resurgence of interest in Yates's writing alongside Stuart O'Nan's preceding retrospective of the author in the *Boston Review*.

I first came across *Revolutionary Road* while working on a novel that was also about marital strife, and it helped me to envisage a route through my material which until then had been unforthcoming. I was gripped by the merciless exactitude with which Yates displayed the everyday disappointments and frustrations of the Wheelers' cohabitation in their 'low-price bracket', 'sweet little house' in 1955, the great spiritual compromise they felt they had made by succumbing to such a life, out in Connecticut expunged from New York, occupying themselves with foursome dinners with their frumpy neighbours Shep and Milly Campbell, who in turn see themselves as somehow cooler, butting up against the edges of dull conventionality, through their association with the glamorous Wheelers ('the girl is *absolutely* ravishing,' the local estate agent Mrs Givings gossips to her husband after meeting them, 'and I think the boy must do something very brilliant in town'). In the Wheelers' and Campbells' bound-together coupledom, their tightly controlled anguish about the widening gap between the youthful idea they hold of themselves and the severely average people they are becoming, I recognised aspects of my own circle

of middle-class thirty-something friends newly accosted by the
needs of their newborns, the accompanying desire for 'nice'
houses in safe neighbourhoods with good schools, and the further accompanying obligation to keep the romance alive at all
costs, that primal, generative factor burdened with the survival
of their family unit.

I read a lot of the novel while sitting on my kitchen floor in
the middle of the day, having abandoned my faltering attempts
to write the novel I was trying to write, and I was struck by the
timelessness and universality of Yates's hopeless vision – for it is
hopeless, ends tragically, the neat nuclear capsule we are encouraged to adopt in our adult lives does not lead to happiness but to
its opposite. It was Yates's scathing, almost demonic honesty
that caught my attention, his precise capturing of the dangerous
vortex of suburbia. 'I don't suppose one picture window is
necessarily going to destroy our personalities,' Frank remarks to
April on viewing the house. It's a quietly hilarious moment,
suggesting an underlying hysteria in the couple's approaching
of their fate.

One piercing domestic detail that has stayed with me since
my first reading of *Revolutionary Road* is Frank's efforts to build a
stone path running from the front door to the road, 'to divert
visitors from coming in through the kitchen'. It is an arduous
task that he returns to without passion during the 'imprisoning'
weekends, and despite his dislike of it, it enfolds him in a theatre
of masculinity that momentarily validates his worth:

> It had seemed simple enough last weekend, when he'd started it,
> but now as the ground sloped off more sharply he found that
> flat stones wouldn't work. He had to make steps, of stones
> nearly as thick as they were wide, stones that had to be dislodged
> from the steep woods behind the house and carried on tottering
> legs around to the front lawn. And he had to dig a pit for each

step, in ground so rocky that it took ten minutes to get a foot below the surface. It was turning into mindless, unrewarding work . . .

Even so, once the first puffing and dizziness was over, he began to like the muscular pull and the sweat of it, and the smell of the earth. At least it was a man's work. At least, squatting to rest on the wooded slope, he could look down and see his house the way a house ought to look on a fine spring day, safe on its carpet of green, the frail white sanctuary of a man's love, a man's wife and children.[28]

The stone path, in its deep-rooted futility, yet so demanding of its maker, is Frank's attempt to concede to what he perceives as the futility of his own existence, and he is rewarded in these episodes with an encouraging reminder of his fundamental role, much more important than any of his quibbling anxieties. With such cruelly, almost laughingly close psychological analysis, Yates applies a stinging relatability to the narrative, its roving scrutiny of household physicality (the picture window 'staring like a big black mirror', the annoying stones) managing to display the human-projected emotional surface of the inanimate. It made me think of my father and his weekend DIY exertions that always made him bad-tempered, and it made me think of the black hole of Sunday afternoons, when the walls seemed to close in, the furniture would take on a hulking, predatory aspect.

I am a little afraid of houses. If you happen to be the product of a troubled childhood, you may tend to avoid its physical manifestation. Bay windows are ugly unwanted pregnancies of glass. A hallway mirror is haunted by broken selves. The semi-detached, the terraced: a line of little warzones of families living side by side, hearing each other's fights and night-time cries. Or the gaping desolation of a garage in winter, or a silent evening driveway. That phrase, 'safe as houses', I have always read as ironic. And the language of houses is rather ominously a patriarchal one: the 'master' bedroom, the 'head' of the table, the 'household', suggesting possession, containment by an iron fist. I think it is possible that the structure in which we are raised never truly lets us go, and if you find yourself as an adult living in a similar structure, there is a chance that you will come to embody or re-enact the past, even its most imposing figure – you are hanging out washing in the garden, and your father within you makes you curse at the dropping of a peg, despite your best efforts never to become your parents. Is it plausible that the architecture of childhood is a template, or a cage, for everything thereafter?

I remember some years ago visiting the just-purchased house of a childhood friend when she was newly married. We had grown up streets away in the same neighbourhood, the north-west London suburbs of Brent, with long back gardens, silent driveways and neat-cut front hedges. My friend had stepped into the sturdy world of marital convention with apparent ease and lightness, a world that I was, then in my twenties, wholly dubious about. On stepping into her new hallway, I had the feeling of entering a dark enclosure, with a faint wickedness to it. Rachel Cusk wrote once, 'Entering a house, I often feel that I am entering a woman's body, and that everything I do there will be felt more intimately by her than by anyone else.'[29] For me it is slightly different. It often feels like entering a male-defined space, in which a woman's core is somehow at risk, by default of being disconnected from herself and therefore losing her power. As I stood in the hallway of my friend's new house, I looked up the stairs into the shadowed mystery of the upper sphere, and it seemed the longest, darkest staircase I had ever seen, with horrors lurking at the top, ready to grasp and swallow. All houses are haunted, by our own ghosts.

Yates created a thorough picture of Frank Wheeler's interior discontent with his suburban cage. We are with him from our first sighting of him in the audience, biting his fist as April humiliates herself playing the lead role in a doomed amateur production of *The Petrified Forest* staged at the local high school. We become acquainted through Yates's masterful exposition with the ugly *Revolutionary Hill* new-builds near the Wheelers' house and the 'clamorous highway called Route Twelve'. Then in the mornings, we join Frank on his train journey into the city to work at the microscopically realised Knox Business Machines, while April stays at home with the children. It was this, *April staying at home with the children*, that I was worried about. That it was happening mostly off the page implied that it bore little narrative interest, and that April, while Frank was at work flirting with his colleague Maureen Grube, did not really exist for those hours as anything more than a prickly, heavy-hipped figment in his mind. But I was deeply, deeply interested in April Wheeler's domestic experience in that house and the impact it was having on her psychology. It was not only of clear dramatic value, but it was the thing with the capacity to have punctured the patriarchal foundation of the novel, its denigration of the literary relevance of female interiority as a significant basis for story. What was the house *doing* to April while Frank was gone? What were the precise colour and texture of the moments that conjured the 'too old and too tall and too intense' woman waiting for Frank at the end of his working day, in place of the 'first-rate girl' he had married?

There are, admittedly, sections in the novel told from April's point of view, one in dialogue as she tells Shep Campbell of her boarding-school years and her life-long 'Emotional Problem' and desire to find a 'sort of heroic super-people' to which she belonged – Shep is only half listening, preoccupied as he is with his desire to sleep with her. There is also a section near the end

of the book, in a chapter written entirely from April's perspective, where we are offered a childhood memory of a visit from
her absent father, but it seems lodged here more as a device to
justify and prepare the reader for her fatal self-inflicted
abortion:

> 'You mean you're – you mean you're not even staying for
> dinner, Daddy?'
>
> 'Sweetie, I'd love to, but I've got these people waiting in
> Boston and they're going to be very, very angry with your
> Daddy if he doesn't get up there in a hurry. How about a kiss?'
>
> And then, hating herself for it, she began acting like a baby.
> 'But you've only stayed about an *hour*. And you – you didn't
> even bring me a present or anything and you—'
>
> 'Oh, *Ape*-rull,' Aunt Claire was saying. 'Why do you want to
> go and spoil a nice visit?'
>
> But at least he wasn't standing up any more: he had squatted
> nimbly beside her and put his arm around her. 'Sweetie, I'm
> afraid you're right about the present, and I feel like a dog about
> it. Listen, though. Tell you what. Let's you and I go out to the
> car and rummage through my stuff, and maybe we can find
> something after all.'[30]

They manage to find, attached to the neck of the White Horse
whisky bottle that April's father carries around in his bag, a tiny
white horse, which he cuts off and gives to her, 'And you can
keep it forever'. It's a bleak, adequately effective memory evoking April's discouraging childhood, yet it is too simplistic and
calculated to grant her the same intimacy of character as that
afforded to her husband. A few pages later she is a casualty, and
we have been invited in this little time we have really spent with
her to feel a great deal of compassion for her. The focus gradually returns to Frank and the rest of the *Revolutionary Road* cast,
and while reading I had no small amount of sympathy for Frank

Wheeler and the new dishevelment of his life, but Yates's writing of him and his comparative underwriting of April is an
example to me of a tendency that can sometimes occur in male
writers to instinctively default to a limited world view shaped
by historic gender inequality. As James Wood has pointed out,
Yates's work is more interested in men than in women, he apparently believed that 'women should have babies and stay at home',
a traditionalist. He was at least cognisant, though, of the destructive entrapment of masculinity, its poison of misplaced power,
and eager to relate this in his fiction.

Books beget other books, as *Madame Bovary* (Yates's favourite
novel) begat *Revolutionary Road*, as *Revolutionary Road* begat
Ordinary People, which was an attempt to colour in the wanting
spaces in a novel that I so loved, to pay equal attention to both
sides of a marital breakdown story. Ensconced at the time in a
similar, if less stark, situation to April Wheeler's (I was working
from home and looking after my children while my partner
went out to work), I found it alarming how deeply the classic
heterosexual parenting roles were ingrained in modern society.
Right from the time of the birth, the father of the child was
barred from the hospital ward overnight, relegating the responsibility of care immediately to the mother. Paternity pay was
subservient to maternity leave and therefore had low take-up, it
made more financial sense for the mother to have the bulk of the
time off in the early months. In addition to this, the UK consistently has the most expensive childcare in the West, deeming
it harder for both parents to sustain their careers on an equal
footing. I saw how easy it could be to fall into the well of convention, how remarkably adhesive those traditional roles
remained, and how naturally this suction could then lead to
relationship disquiet, disconnection from the self, loss of identity, and the four walls, the furniture, the house itself, taking on
that predatory aspect so befitting of the gothic.

Another important factor, before *Revolutionary Road*, that contributed to the conception of *Ordinary People* was a news story I came across about the death of Catherine Bailey, a successful lawyer and mother of three who jumped off Richmond Bridge into the Thames in the summer of 2009, not long after the birth of her third child. News reports said that she was struggling to balance the demands of motherhood with her job, that she was suffering from post-partum depression. Nobody knows exactly what Catherine Bailey was feeling, the colours and the textures, but the fact of her tragedy is crucial to remember, how the demands made on women's lives amid the pillars of history and progress in a rampantly capitalist society can come to feel crushing or insurmountable. 'Write exactly what happened,' Yates says of the charge of fiction. Even when we don't know what happened, write the truth of it as precisely, as faithfully as possible, and you may be required to invent the attire and the event of that truth, but never the core of it. That is what we are doing when we tell stories: nailing truth. I keep that piece of paper on my wall of Yates's wretched writing cocoon to remind me of the necessity of the work.

James Baldwin: Why Beale Street Still Talks

James Baldwin never goes out of fashion. This might seem an enviable attribute for a writer to sustain posthumously, if it were not for one of the significant reasons why. He's a soldier, a comrade. He is a brother-in-arms in a war that doesn't end. Along with Toni Morrison, Angela Davis, Richard Wright, Nina Simone, Langston Hughes, Maya Angelou and many others, he is among those foremost in a longstanding army of artists and activists who have challenged, fought and assuaged racism and become icons of the ongoing struggle for black equality. As the struggle continues, and does not appear to be concluding any time soon, Baldwin's work is as relevant and as prevailing as ever.

The latest landmark in the ever-building homage and salutation to Baldwin's writing is Oscar-winning Barry Jenkins's adaptation of his penultimate novel *If Beale Street Could Talk*. Set in Harlem in the 1970s, it's a mournful, limpid, at times excruciating portrayal of an engaged young couple, Fonny and Tish (played by Stephan James and KiKi Layne), who are separated by Fonny's sudden incarceration after being falsely accused of rape, leaving Tish to weather pregnancy alone. The film successfully mirrors the book's oscillating, dreamy atmosphere, capturing the childlike innocence of Tish's love-soaked narrative voice which accentuates the cruelty of the world around them. She asks, late in the novel, Fonny still hopelessly imprisoned and childbirth close, 'What happened here? surely, this land is cursed.'

The land she is referring to, of course, is America. And

approaching fifty years on, it may indeed still appear so, floundering as it is in the grip of a dubious populist presidency, its sprays of government-tolerated mass shootings, its ever-growing collection of dead black men and women. One of the most chilling moments in Jenkins's adaptation of *Beale Street* is a confrontation that occurs between Fonny and the police officer who gets him sent down, Officer Bell. His eyes seethe with hatred; he has a stiff, Nazi strut, and he could easily be reimagined walking straight off set to play the starring role in any random police killing on contemporary US soil (Eric Garner, Michael Brown, Tanisha Anderson, Freddie Gray, Alton Sterling, Aura Rosser, Walter Scott, the list goes on). This stark resemblance to our time is also what makes Raoul Peck's unflinching 2016 documentary about Baldwin, *I Am Not Your Negro*, even more difficult to watch: here the footage of baton-beatings and the sad dark photographs of long-ago lynchings are real, and what's more, the sentiment behind those lynchings seems far from quashed.

Jenkins had already written the *Beale Street* script well before he released *Moonlight*, the Oscar-crowned film that made his name, citing Baldwin as his 'personal school of life'. Ta-Nehisi Coates used the epistolary address of Baldwin's seminal essay volume *The Fire Next Time* as a template for his stirring, National Book Award-winning memoir *Between the World and Me*, and in 2017 Jesmyn Ward edited and published a collection of essays on race in modern America called *The Fire This Time*, underscoring how pertinent that text remains. No one else articulates with quite the same inexhaustible clarity the outrage, hardship and fury of existing on the receiving end of the construct of race, the sense of being endangered, at best truncated, both physically and spiritually, on a most fundamental level. It is a state of being that crosses global boundaries and whose ramifications are manifold and timeless, deeming

Baldwin a classic, universal voice, cherished and held close by millions. His writing usually makes me cry, his perfect use of a careful word, the way he uses colons, the way he uses position-ing and repetition and pattern, how all of it manifests in a shrewd, precise expression of a victimised yet triumphant humanity. One of my favourite descriptions in *If Beale Street Could Talk* is Tish's image of Fonny and his friends: 'They were always coming down the street, in rags, bleeding, full of lumps.' There is a disarming immediacy in that phrase, 'coming down the street', it is slightly colloquial, vague and exact at the same time, evoking so many groups of young black men coming down so many streets, like soldiers, armed with an inner humour and defiance and the tightly held tenderness of those, like Tish, who love them, lumps and all.

Born in New York in 1924, Baldwin grew up in poverty in Harlem, the eldest of nine children, and was a gifted Pentecostal preacher prior to becoming a writer, though he eventually left the church, deeming it a reinforcement of institutionalised modes of oppression. A novelist, essayist, playwright and short-story writer, during his lifetime he occupied the position of a kind of literary spokesman for the civil-rights movement, appearing on the cover of *Time* magazine in 1963 and forming friendships with Malcolm X, Martin Luther King and Medgar Evers, all of whom were assassinated within a five-year span, which he was trying to address in his unfinished manuscript 'Remember This House', the basis for *I Am Not Your Negro*. 'His writing became polemical,' the American author and critic Hilton Als noted,[31] having curated an exhibition of photog-raphy of Baldwin at the David Zwirner Gallery in New York, depicting the writer in private moments, with family and friends, beyond the clamour of his almost messianic public per-sona. Entitled *God Made My Face: A Collective Portrait of James Baldwin*, the show is an attempt to 'give him back to himself', after effectively being stolen by the harsh and urgent lights of the ongoing cause he found himself fighting for, an unavoidable cause, standing directly in the path, not just of his survival, but of his ability to create. 'I have not written about being a Negro at such length because I expect that to be my only subject,' Baldwin wrote in *Notes of a Native Son*, 'but only because it was the gate I had to unlock before I could hope to write about anything else.'

Baldwin's characters are varied, immediate and closely imagined. In a prolific stream of stories and novels – *Giovanni's Room, Another Country, Go Tell It on the Mountain, Just Above My Head* – he inhabits the psychologies of the people in his narratives with a seemingly boundless reach of compassion, ascribing to Henry James's assertion in *The Art of Fiction*, 'the province of art is all life, all feeling, all observation, all vision'. Yet he grappled throughout his career with the imposition, the imprisonment, of race, his craftsmanship being, if not upstaged, at least manoeuvred by its implicit activism, a little like his friend Nina Simone who deep down just really wanted to be a classical pianist but also found herself a soldier, battling a force with her music that jeopardised the music itself, changed it, moulded it, and perhaps even, by a default of fury, made it greater. Blackness claimed them with its trouble, and its insidious lie that that trouble belonged only to blackness. It is the same lie that perpetually, almost unthinkingly, affixes the theme of race to the work of black writers whether or not they choose to write about race, implying that the work of white or non-black writers is not also about race, when of course it is, in the luxury of its apparent absence that has been made possible by racism. Race is like air, we all breathe it, but the long-held assumption is that the 'black struggle' is somehow self-contained, that it is not a world struggle, a peace-call, a societal imbalance in which all of us are implicated and for which we are all responsible.

This is akin to what Baldwin was referring to in his hope for 'a moral change' in America, which he did not see in his lifetime: an acknowledgement of how the subjugation of blackness has facilitated the relative comfort of whiteness, how the imprisoned have sustained the free. 'Not once have the Civilized been able to honor, recognize, or describe the Savage,'[32] he wrote in 1984, three years before his death. 'He is, practically speaking, the source of their wealth, his continued subjugation the key to their power and glory.' Unwilling to accept the impact of this injustice on his life and on his writing (he once said in an interview with the poet Nikki Giovanni that he could never write when he was in his hometown of New York), Baldwin lived for many years in southern France in a self-imposed exile, but America and its 'Negro problem' remained at the epicentre of his work. He was inseparable from it. It was inside him, and in making his art he was manifesting, insisting upon his freedom within it, even as he was still imprisoned. Did he ever fully open that gate and walk through to the other side of what seemed possible? I sense that he did, just from the way he uses colons, the audaciousness and certainty in those little decisions he made in those particular moments, in the full possession of language.

If Baldwin were alive today, it is doubtful that he would detect enough of the moral change that he was looking for. He might instead wearily go to his typewriter and sit down and write a story about an Eric Garner or another real-life Fonny. Or he might read his harrowing 'Going To Meet The Man', the closing short story in the 1965 collection of the same title, which is a story that I will never forget reading and will read again and again to help me remember the luxury of my own liberty. He might re-read this story of a little boy on a family outing to watch a neighbourhood lynching, and he might shake his head at how a writer could write such a horrific story and then fifty years later come back and write another story maybe not so very different from it. He might think that, given this, it will never be possible for anyone to really be free, of the past, and of the obligation to activism, be it inside or outside of our art.

Financial Times, 2019

Bernardine Evaristo on *The Emperor's Babe*

As a young writer, stuck on a novel, I attended a weekend workshop run by Bernardine Evaristo, on the theme of fusing poetry with fiction. I considered myself not quite a poet and not quite a fiction writer, and was aiming for a form somewhere in between. It was a small group. Evaristo was powerful and kind. She led us through a series of writing and characterisation exercises, there were discussions and readings from work we'd produced. After the workshop she took me aside and offered to act as a mentor through the writing of my novel, a pivotal act of generosity that aided the eventual completion of *26a*, and taught me that writing is not just a solitary pursuit; it is also about community.

Over her extensive career, Evaristo has helped many other writers, both through personal mentoring and broader institutional initiatives aimed at creating more opportunity for writers of colour, such as the Evaristo Prize for African Poetry (formerly named Brunel International African Poetry Prize) and The Complete Works poetry scheme. She is a literary activist in the most dynamic sense of the word, helping to achieve real change on the artistic landscape as well as broadening the audience for poetry, and none of this at an expense to the accomplishments of her own work. She is a writer — poet-novelist, prose stylist, fiction-fusionist, dramatist, essayist — of huge range and swagger, who has buoyantly maintained a commitment to experimentalism and adventure in her practice without bowing to the pressures of the market. My two favourites of her novels are the Booker Prize-winning *Girl, Woman,*

Other and *The Emperor's Babe*, a guzzling, groundbreaking, multi-linguistic triumph of literary play and outright *zing*, which remains one of the best things I've ever read.

When *The Emperor's Babe* was published in 2001, partly a result of a residency Evaristo had undertaken at the Museum of London, I interviewed her for an article about her work in a mainstream broadsheet, at a time when it was still relatively rare for the national press to give significant interview space to British writers of colour who were not bestsellers or major prize-winners. We talked in the front room of her flat in west London, from which she had recently thrown out her TV to avoid the distraction it posed to her writing and her mind. The novel, which imagined the life of a black woman in Roman London, continued Evaristo's exploration of history that she had begun in her first verse novel, *Lara*, in which she delved into her family ancestry which spans England, Ireland, Germany, Nigeria and Brazil. In 2019's *Girl, Woman, Other*, after forays into prose novels such as *Blonde Roots* and *Mr Loverman*, Evaristo brilliantly returned to her natural fusionist mode and continued the project of writing black women into both historical and contemporary British life. On the night she won the Booker Prize, several of us 'sister writers' were gathered in a bar in Mayfair to watch the ceremony on-screen. When her name was announced (controversially alongside Margaret Atwood's), there was euphoria. It was right that she had won it, wrong that it had taken so long for a black woman to win it, right that she was the one to do so – a moment of divine justice.

After this interview, in which we talked in depth about the writing of *The Emperor's Babe*, Evaristo showed me a vision board that she had created of her hopes for her career. Everything on it appears to have come true since then, which is a testament to the role of positive thinking in setting goals and sustaining a long career, something she has always held in great sway. Early on in the conversation, she described at length the inspiration behind *The Emperor's Babe* with the same upbeat energy, the same attitude of inner drive and creative delight: 'My interest for quite a while has been the exploration of British history through fiction,' she said, 'looking at the black presence in Britain, and also Europe, through the ages, the stories that haven't been told. I discovered a long time ago in Peter Fryer's book *Staying Power: The History of Black People in Britain*, that Africans had been based at Hadrian's Wall during the Roman occupation, at the beginning of the third century AD (the earliest recorded date of the black presence in Britain). This sparked my imagination – I found it amazing that black people were in England 1,800 years ago, when many of us think we only arrived here in the twentieth century, predominantly on the *Windrush*. I wanted to imagine a black woman living in Roman London, and I thought I'd choose a character who was Egyptian because the Romans colonised Egypt, as they did much of North Africa, but then I thought people might visualise her as Mediterranean-looking, whereas I wanted them to imagine a very dark-skinned black woman in Roman London, which makes more of a statement, rather than a character who resembled the Hollywood portrayal of, say, Cleopatra. That's why I decided to locate her family origins beyond Egypt into ancient Nubia where people are very dark (now Northern Sudan and Southern Egypt).'

When Evaristo told people she was writing a novel-in-verse about a black woman in Roman London, 'It was a real conversation-stopper.' The idea may have seemed of little interest to some, but it allowed her to delve into Britain's long multicultural history, filling a hole in the wide gaps of public knowledge surrounding it. 'Two thousand years ago the Romans occupied England for four hundred years. After they left, we were conquered by the Saxons, Vikings and Normans, and from the fifteenth century people came in from Africa,

primarily through the slave trade. By 1596 there were so many
black people in Britain that Queen Elizabeth I issued a special
commandment that they be "discharged out of Her Majesty's
dominions". In the eighteenth century, London had a significant
population of black people estimated at between ten and fifteen
thousand, many of them formerly enslaved, who had fought on
the British side during the American Revolution and been
granted freedom in England as their reward. Britain has always
been multicultural. Irish and Jewish people settled in London
from at least the twelfth century. Flemish, German, Italian and
Spanish merchants arrived in medieval times, and by the mid-
sixteenth century there were Dutch, German and French
protestants, Americans and Australians who arrived from the
seventeenth century. There were Chinese in Stepney in the
eighteenth century, Indians in the nineteenth century. So this is
a hybrid history and today's multicultural society is simply a
continuation of what it's always been. The myth of Britishness
is that it's white and monocultural, and that suddenly in 1948
black people arrived and later Asian people and we started to
become this mongrel race. That's simply not true. Even when
you look within the demography of these shores and isles, there
are Irish, Welsh, Scots, Manx and Cornish nations and regions
with their own languages.'

Keen, then, to point out the commonalities in the nature of
our origins, Evaristo is also of the opinion that writers of colour
should not bear a direct responsibility for writing race, 'because
that is limiting us, implying that it's the defining feature in our
lives. There are many aspects to our lives and racism is just one
of them, which impacts on each of us very differently.' In *The
Emperor's Babe*, she is not writing race at all, in fact, because anti-
black racism did not exist in Roman times. 'Anti-black racism
evolved, or at least was accelerated, as an ideology to justify the
slave trade. The ancient Romans had their prejudices and viewed

those who weren't Romans as barbarians, but it wasn't related to skin colour or African cultures. In writing about Zuleika, a black girl living in Roman London, I'm not writing about racism because it wasn't relevant then, yet racist and colonial ideology underpins how British history has been recorded. In one section of the book, I do use the Roman Empire as a metaphor for the British Empire. There is so much more than racism for we British writers of the African diaspora to explore.'

History was Evaristo's favourite subject at school, partly sparked by a curiosity about her Nigerian father's background. While researching the novel, she read some fifty books, using the Museum of London residency to enrich her understanding of what Roman London was like. 'The Museum had a permanent life-size exhibition that recreated several Roman rooms and shops, which was very helpful to me in trying to imagine people's everyday lives at that time. It made me realise how modern Roman culture was in many ways – for example, the Roman kitchen in the museum reminded me of a contemporary rustic kitchen. The obvious sophistication of the Roman culture influenced the anachronistic mash-up I employ in *The Emperor's Babe*, where the past and present are blurred. This strategy helped me make the fictional world I create feel very present and dynamic, and the characters as vivid and relatable as if they were people living today. I wanted people to imagine historical London through contemporary London, and contemporary London through historical London, which is why I gave the different areas of Roman London contemporary street names so that people could locate how the current city is overlaid on the ancient one. The research was wholly absorbing and fascinating. It gave me many ideas for the novel, such as discovering that the Romans had central heating, they had poetry societies, they had orgies, same-sex relationships (this was pre-Christianity so there was no shame attached to same-sex relationships), they had

cross-dressers. My characters wear Versace, Gucci and Armani –
it was very convenient that some of the most well-known
fashion names are Italian – and there are also internet references
in the novel. Overall, I was occupied with reinterpretation and
thinking about this history imaginatively, because it had long
been clear to me that the writing of history is not objective.
People focus on versions of the past, which are then presented as
history. So many other aspects of the past, such as women, the
working classes and other marginalised communities, have been
excluded from the official timelines.'

One of the things I love most about this particular novel is
the sheer confidence and flamboyance of its concoction: the
poky vegetable shop where Zuleika is plucked from her struggling family into a life of luxury as wife to a hideous nobleman,
her best friend Alba's comedic balance of dignity and promiscu-
ity, and a cross-dressing prostitute named Venus who completes
the feisty threesome. Was an element of this confidence born
from the prior exclusion of such material from history, I wondered, offering the freedom to create your own narrative, your
own language – there are a lot of interesting linguistics at play
in the book, like 'wassup', 'stylee' and 'sweet FA'? 'I think it's
about giving myself the permission to express my narrative as I
see fit, and people will either like it or they won't,' Evaristo said.
'The city in my novel is culturally heterogenous and the languages, phrases and words include Patois, Latin, modern Italian,
Scots, slang, even Americanisms. I gave myself the freedom to
throw all of that into the mix and stir it up a little, also making
up compound words which are a mixture of English and Latin.
The English language itself is heteroglot so again it's simply a
continuation of what has always been. Through this experiment, I aimed to bring the characters to life and to enrich the
text by alluding to contemporary society through language
itself. You know, Zuleika speaks a "second-generation plebby

creole", which mirrors black people in Britain of my generation who speak a mixture of Patois and English. With regard to the Latin, words came into my head quite naturally, which I then exploited. It helped that I had studied Latin for five years at school. And because I was intent on capturing everyday speech, modern vernacular and slang emerged. All of these components weren't premeditated but happened organically, which for me is the magic of the creative process. I start writing unsure of what will emerge, and when the writing is going well, I'm excited and surprised at what materialises on the page.'

When asked if she laughed a lot while writing *The Emperor's Babe*, for it's a uniquely funny book, Evaristo replied that she did, 'I kept giggling . . . it was a lot of fun to write.' Her first book was the poetry collection *Island of Abraham,* followed by the semi-autobiographical novel-in-verse *Lara.* Poetry has always been a foundational element of her work – her favourite poet as a teenager was Dylan Thomas, though she reveals that she is not much influenced by traditional forms of poetry. 'I think the issue of poetry is a very interesting one,' she said. 'Poetry as a subject in schools has a lot to answer for as it's been very effective in destroying most people's interest in it. Most people, when you talk about poetry, start getting palpitations because they see it as something very dense and obscure and out of their reach; something they can't relate to. I think we need to think of poetry having multiple functions and reaching different kinds of audiences – it can be engaging and readable, lively, nuanced, subtle, layered, deep and also accessible. I don't think poetry has to be obscure for it to be valued. I don't want my readers approaching this novel with dread because it's poetry, but instead to be open to being taken on a wild ride.'

Evaristo grew up in Woolwich, south London, the fourth of eight children in a mixed-race family – her mother was an English teacher and her father a welder – 'we had no money'. For four of her primary-school years she went to a local convent school, then for her secondary education to a girls' school in Eltham, after which she trained as an actress. As a child she loved reading, 'perhaps because I come from a large family. Reading was a way of escaping from everybody without having to leave the house; so you're sitting in a room full of nine other people and you could get stuck in a book and just shut them out. Also, I was very shy at one stage in my life when I was a teenager, and I used to walk to school reading a book. So I've always loved literature.' From the age of fourteen, though, she wanted to be an actress, having discovered that 'if I stood on stage acting, I'd get lots of attention and people would clap for me'. After drama school she worked in theatre for several years and was routinely writing her own material, preferring it to performing in other people's plays. 'The joy of writing your own material is that it's your voice, your choices, your storytelling. I fell out of love with acting in the end. I wasn't a natural performer and it became an ordeal.'

The plays Evaristo wrote at drama school were partly a result of the dearth of material in the college library featuring black characters: 'I couldn't find any.' Her own material mostly took the form of monologues and dramatic plays, designed for performance, which appears to have impacted her later writing – her creation of characters, for instance, their distinctive voices and personalities that leap off the page. She lays claim to 'a streak of exhibitionism' herself, rumbling beneath that early shyness, and which first found a home at a local youth theatre she attended as a teenager, once released there by her father's strictness, deeming it an acceptable place for passing the time. 'My father didn't really allow us out of the house much. I think he was frightened that it was a big bad world out there, especially because he was an African immigrant – he wanted to protect us. He knew that "nice children" went to the youth theatre, so I was allowed to go and socialise there from the age of twelve.' It is fitting that some four decades after her acting training, Evaristo is now President of her alma mater Rose Bruford College in Kent alongside her many other accolades, an example of a career equal in creative achievement and giving back.

Following the Booker Prize win, a few sister writers gathered with Evaristo to celebrate at a London restaurant. She brought along her positive-thinking advice – the vision board, the affirmations, the goal-setting – which she wanted to share with us to assist us on our own journeys, maybe to a similar peak. Her reaction to success is to share its secret and spread possibility, reinforcing the idea of art as activism and community, you take the community with you, however high you reach. Ultimately the writing itself is where success is to be found: whether you have progressed, whether you are sustaining your faith in its value, whether you are keeping on going, no matter what. 'I want to always be growing as a writer. Each book should be a development on the last one, and different. I take risks with my novels. It's important to always develop your craft, to read as widely as possible and of course to learn from other writers.'

© Diana Evans, 2024

All the Notes

It was Jackie Collins who said, 'Start with as little as possible.'
I wrote this down on a Post-it note because I wanted to remember it. She was referring to the question of how to begin a
novel. Not with reams of notes, box files of research, a detailed
plan. But with almost nothing. That way, went the notion,
you have open space to dive into your story; ideas, surprise
routes and the unexpected can emerge, you are free of the
constraints of exaggerated premeditation, it is just you and the
blank page. I wanted to remember this because I recognised its
rightness – there *should* be as little as possible between mind
and matter in the act of writing – and also because starting
with little is something I find difficult. I tend to start with a
lot. Notes and notes and notes, a box of them, on stray bits of
paper, old receipts, torn pieces of kitchen towel. Add to that
marked journal snippets and random thoughts and phrases
from notebooks: 'apple orchard, grey birds, a stream flowing
by'. I don't always know what the notes mean or what they are
referring to, but I understand that in the moment of their
writing, they were imperative and urgent, in case they might
one day belong to something, or they already did, such as the
novel I was about to write. Or maybe it was just a need to
record a particular moment of being alive, which speaks to the
fundamental purpose of fiction.

'As little as possible' is the utopia that escapes me at the
beginnings of my journeys (I do not travel light). And I have
noticed that as time goes on, it recedes further into

impossibility. At first, I had just two notebooks. One was for writing down quotes that I liked from books that I was reading (Audre Lorde: 'poetry is the way we help give name to the nameless so it can be thought';[33] Mary Oliver: 'how I would like/to have wings –/blue ones –/ribbons of flame'[34]). The other was for recording moments, images, impressions that I didn't want to forget, which is a routine pastime for a writer, so after twenty years of writing fiction there are now several of these 'observational' notebooks, a backlist. But there are, in addition, other notebooks, with different functions: There is the notebook for note-taking on books that I am reading – what I am learning from them, what ideas for my own work are emerging while reading them. This is distinct, importantly, from the quote book that I have already mentioned, and after decades of reading, this latter type also has a backlist, a pile of them on my shelf next to a row of books on writing craft. Then there is the notebook for the jotting down of ideas for stories and drafting out rough plans and passages for works-in-progress. Another notebook for lists of books I plan to read and films I want to see. At one point recently, I thought it might be useful to have a 'project notebook', to accompany the writing of a novel, but thankfully this didn't work for me; I like a certain amount of messiness in the novel-writing process and don't like to feel that it is capable of being contained within two covers.

That is now four notebooks. There is another for everyday work jottings, to-do lists, etc. The sixth, with the biggest backlist of all, is my journal, in which anything and everything might be recorded. Here is the rawest truth that sometimes creeps into my stories or dominates them entirely. It is often where beginnings can be found, a seed that can be drawn out and expanded away from its source. For example, observing my mother during a walk:

An aroma of mint makes her pause and inspect, or if we talk about something that particularly engages her she will stop where she is and raise her head, looking skyward. We pass the green. The sky is dense and still. She has a Sunday swagger as if she owns the neighbourhood.

This was later developed and used in a novel. The recording of immediate experience or reflection in a blank space where nothing is expected of it is freeing for the mind and good for the craft. I have noticed, though, that the more I write with intention, be it fiction or non-fiction, the less I am called to the journal, unless I am experiencing an extremity of emotion or revelation or there is a glimmer of something that must be captured, such as an expression on the face of someone close to you in which their deepest vulnerability becomes clear and it momentarily breaks your heart. The journal is distinct from a diary: it is for the preserving of thought and feeling rather than event.

Six categories of notebook. These multiple depositories make me wonder whether there is cause for concern. Is it a sign of some ailing internal deconstruction? A self becoming compartmentalised and losing hold of its core? Does every thought now require a place to lodge? And does this requirement mean that thoughts are truncated by anxious forethought, only half formed? What happens to the thoughts that want to simply exist without consequence and fleet, and disappear? In her novel *The Golden Notebook*, Doris Lessing charted a woman's psychological breakdown through the use of five colour-coded notebooks: red, for Anna Wulf's experiences as a member of the communist party; blue, for her personal memories, dreams and emotions; yellow, for the recording of a dissipating love affair; black, for her time in Zimbabwe (then Rhodesia) before and during World War II. The fifth, the golden notebook, was the resolution, the attempt to restore wholeness to a fragmented personality. I suppose a version of my golden notebook could be the journal, but my developing distance from it further suggests a possible disconnection from the centre.

I have come instead, of late, to quite rely on the Post-it note – those luminous, non-committal, assorted squares of bright concision on which can be written a pressing thought, a piece of dialogue so accurate to its character that if it is not recorded it feels like a little death, or just a reminder to buy eggs. The Post-its have a sense of liberty about them, being unattached in being unbound, they negate categorisation. I keep a block of them on my desk, on the bedside table, in the kitchen, so that I am able in almost any moment to hold on to the hurtling flow of messages from the brain, perhaps to avoid being washed away. Everywhere I look there are these random psychedelic squares of instruction, reminding me of Russell Crowe's portrayal of John Nash in the film *A Beautiful Mind* – the scrawlings on the walls, the chaos of scattered paper. Perhaps the notebooks will become defunct and the Post-its will take over. They require no allegiance, no preceding decision or classification on my part (where does this thought *belong*? which list, which colour?). They are uncontainable, like a woman's life.

At the beginning of writing a novel, then, there is the opposite of as little as possible. Jackie Collins is of no use to me. For novels are like sea lions. They slip from your grasp. They jump off distant rocks and make big splashes that catch your clothes and make you feel it, the whole thing, the thing that you are trying to capture. When you try to reach out and grasp it, it dives under, takes off, laughs at you, peeps at you when you're becoming desperate, with something like sympathy, but retreats again when you walk up close. It does not want to be captured. It wants to live its life in peace.

And so I make notes, to keep me connected to the story. I keep them in a box with a lid and look at them when I am lost. But you can make too many notes when you are lost, and cling to them too tightly. Once, during a long writing project, my sea lion was on the floor, groaning. He was plastered to my laminate with little neatly arranged pieces of paper containing lists and buzzwords indicating what was in each chapter. He didn't like it there at all. I had to let him go and accept that I was lost, and wait for him to splash me again. Is too much better than too little? Is everything better than nothing?

My fourth novel, *A House for Alice*, began its life with one such lidded box inherited from the writing of the previous novel, *Ordinary People*, during which it had become necessary for such a box to exist. In it were kept the random Post-its and scraps of paper collected in my thinking and living. You are walking through Tesco looking for lightbulbs and something smashes to the floor by itself – you must write it down. Or you are making okra stew while listening to Wizkid and a voice in your head starts talking about when Choice FM got taken over by Capital Radio 'and they started calling it Capital Xtra? You think I don't care about that?' she says – and you must immediately write *this* down on a Post-it because when the book (in this case Nicole from *A House for Alice*) is talking to you, you must pay attention, otherwise it might turn away. Hilary Mantel described the frenzy of note-gathering as becoming a magpie, 'Collect anything that attracts you: images, phrases, little glimpses, footnotes from books.'[35] The books too, other books, are part of the thinking. I found a solid root of *A House for Alice* in Eugene O'Neill's *Long Day's Journey Into Night*, and other flickers in Colm Toibin's *Brooklyn* and Derek Walcott's poetry. *Ordinary People* would probably not exist without John Updike's *Couples*, Tolstoy's *War and Peace* and Claire Messud's *The Emperor's Children*. All the books, all the notebooks, all the

Post-its and scraps in the box, they are all present, asking to be accounted for.

It is difficult, dangerous to sea lions, getting the scraps and snippets to find their places. It can feel like maths instead of English, a staggering process of finding the right equations or puzzle of arrangement. I was not fond of maths in school, and when writing starts to feel like maths I begin to wish to be the kind of novelist who sits down to write with nothing pre-existing, no notion of where they are going – although the idea of this, of having no idea of destination, fills me with a nauseating dread: I must *know*, if not at the beginning of draft one, then at the outset of another draft further down the line. In the early drafting of *Ordinary People*, I had some shreds of this overly repetitive passage, which for a long time was all I had, a paperweight, the only solid thing that I knew belonged in the novel, and it was just barely enough to keep going:

> The frescos in the Italian court were fading . . . The tombs in the Egyptian court were opening . . . The tiles in the Moorish court were falling. The dinosaurs in the gardens were yawning . . . The deities in the Grecian court were eroding. The Sphinxes at the entrance were corroding. The birds in the aviaries were wailing. The skies of Pissarro were darkening . . . The keys of the grand piano were breaking. The steps of the grand entrance . . .

I had no idea where it belonged, this clumsy tumbling of notes, this repeated rhythm of objects falling and eroding. The writing, over the next five (of seven) years, was a search for the right place to put it, which turned out to be about four-fifths of the way through the novel, near the end. For a long time it felt like maths, and was very unpleasant. There were three Januarys of rewriting chapter one. When I finally found where that strange passage belonged, it was one of the most electrifying things I have ever experienced, part relief, part thrilling excitement. It was a hazardous neatness of a spark arriving at a place to fizz. It was a herd of sea lions swimming into shore with bells on their noses. Afterwards I went for a long drive and the air was trembling, the streets whizzing by. Although the novel was not yet finished, I knew that it one day would be, which until then had not been certain. Writing is a high-risk pursuit.

Crucially, though, not all the notes will find their places. Some do not belong and only exist as part of a current. The secret is in managing the notes. You must not try to force them to belong – something I have found myself guilty of, the clutching of the darlings – because you threaten to disrupt the balance, be it of chapters, of passages, or even the entirety. The utopia I aspire to now is not to begin with nothing, but to locate in yourself the bravery to leave the notes behind, trusting that their usefulness is embedded in the ink of your pen, without heaviness or insistence.

I remember arriving at such a place while working on my first novel, *26a*. I had taken myself away to America to a women's writing retreat called Hedgebrook, situated on Whidbey Island off the coast of Seattle. I was given a cottage in the woods in which to live and work for two months, the first few days of which were spent in a cushioned corner in my cottage leafing through my notes, thinking, reading, worrying. At some point, brought about by my gradual settling there and the distance from familiarity, by the chance to talk in the evenings with other women who were also trying to write, a new freedom surfaced and slowly grew bigger. It was like swimming out into the water I had crossed by boat to get there, on the last leg of my journey. I began to write, and the notes were newly somewhere behind me, hanging around by themselves or talking in huddles, they had loosened their hold on me, acquired an irrelevance that pushed me forward. Leave the notes behind, and the maths will disappear.

The final and most important thing of all to make note of here is that there are no rules to writing. The 'show don't tell', the tenets of the limited or omniscient point of view, the 'road to hell is paved with adverbs', the 'too long sentence', the 'too many adjectives', the avoidance of repetition in favour of precision or George Orwell's clear window pane. I like the freedom of using the word blue twice in one sentence if it reads brightly. I like a sentence to run on to whole paragraphs and make grammar play with its infinite tools. The point is that no one can tell us anything about how to be who we are, we have to find out for ourselves, with as much or as little as we can carry. To remind myself of the place in the woods where I found the way to leave the notes behind, I brought back some notes, which I consult when needed. Such as:

Think of images before words for description.
Follow yourself and not the hours. Exist outside of time.
I know that I am most at peace when I am writing. In it there are alleyways to being free.

© Diana Evans, 2024

At Toni Church

The day of the announcement of Toni Morrison's death, I sat down on my stair and wept. There was a new gap on the landscape. We had never met, I had never interviewed her, but it felt like a closer loss than that of a stranger. Something of Toni Morrison resided in us from afar, in that we found ourselves so thoroughly, so recognised and so commonplace in her work. Yet she made no crusade to save or rescue us in particular. Her devotion was foremost to her art: 'What I cannot face is living without my art,' she wrote in 'The Foreigner's Home', collected in *Mouth Full of Blood*. 'I come from a group of people who have always refused to live that way. In the fields we would not live without it. In chains we would not live without it – and we lived historically in the country without *everything*, but not without our music, not without our art.' She wrote for the folk, of the folk, never colluded in our exclusion from what was considered worthy of depiction, while at the same time never allowed herself, in the act of creation, her very delight in it, to be imposed upon.

In the weeks following her death, there were events, gatherings, public and private salutations in the church of Toni Morrison. I took part in one such event at the Southbank Centre in London, where a panel of writers discussed the impact and importance of her work. The audience was weepy and confessional, ready with their Toni stories, the books they favoured (*Beloved* and *The Bluest Eye* seem generally the most loved; my favourite is *Song of Solomon*), the deep respect they held for the life she had so brilliantly lived. People stood up in the pews to speak. A screening was watched of the 2019 documentary made about Morrison's work and life, *Toni Morrison: The Pieces I Am*, where there is that wonderful story she relates of the moment she realised that she was happy, and saw the character Beloved from the novel walking towards her out of the river behind her back porch, wearing a hat.

Like many of us who call ourselves writers, I have always been awed by Toni Morrison, her occupation of a literary zenith I imagine myself incapable of reaching. It's true that a Morrison sentence contains a sole and formidable mystery, they come from an inimitable mind, a wellspring assembled from a particular gathering of experience, vision, instinct and spiritual and intellectual energy. Her work is also, of course, of the American landscape, geographical and historical, and concerned with the social and political experience of African Americans at the hands of race and racism. I have found her overarching project a useful paradigm of how literature can be a change-making force against sites of political exploitation, the pain caused to the interior life in its shaping of the corresponding exterior circumstance. For it is the same pain, the same condition of subjugation, in which sense the project is a universal one. Interestingly, there have been occasions in my contact with readers when the characters in my novels have been referred to as 'African American', or when some dubiousness has been expressed about the relevance of documenting, for example, the election of Barack Obama in a British novel, as if the two worlds were unrelated.

The most pivotal union I have found with Morrison in my own writing is in her desire and attempt to deconstruct race, to highlight the existence of its everyday language while declothing herself of it, and searching instead for a new chamber of communication. 'If I have to live in a racial house,' she writes in the essay 'Race Matters', 'it was important at the least to rebuild it so that it was not a windowless prison into which I was forced, a thick-walled, impenetrable container from which no sound could be heard, but rather an open house, grounded, yet generous in its supply of windows and doors.' I thought of this imperative all through the writing of *A House for Alice*, a novel that is preoccupied with the concept of home as a site of internal conflict and loss, and also of fantasy and dreaming, questioning the notion that it is possible to belong anywhere more fully or more safely than to the self. At the heart of Morrison's oeuvre is the gift of great storytelling, fuelled by an ulterior motive of pursuing justice, and neither at the expense of the other. 'I could strike out for new territory,' she intended, 'to find a way to free my imagination of the impositions and limitations of race *and* explore the consequences of its centrality in the world and in the lives of the people I was hungry to write about.'[36]

Five months before her death in the summer of 2019, *A Mouth Full of Blood* was published in the UK, for which I wrote the following recollections in the *Sunday Times*.

★

When I was an undergraduate at university, there were three black women across the Atlantic whom I considered my friends, in the way that books and their authors can often seem. Their names were Toni Morrison, Alice Walker and Maya Angelou. They were the pre-eminence of a virtual global sisterhood that voiced the collective souls of us girls stranded amid everyday diasporic alienation, patriarchy and white feminism. Alice was quiet and loved flowers and had a kind of angelic mist around her. Maya was flamboyant and sassy and tall and red-lipsticked. And Toni was imperious, with her silver-dreaded crown, her magnanimous ghostly melodrama and lightning intellect, like a haughty aunty who could slap you down with a single exquisite sentence.

There were other friends too: June Jordan, Audre Lorde, bell hooks, Nella Larson, Zora Neale Hurston, Toni Cade Bambara. They were mostly Americans, to begin with, and the ones with the loudest plaudits got the most attention – Walker and Morrison both won Pulitzers, for *The Color Purple* and *Beloved* respectively, and Morrison was awarded the Nobel Prize in Literature in 1993. But it wasn't the plaudits that made me cherish these women. It was the stories they told and the way they told them, with a kind of warm power, and the people inside those pages whom I didn't see much of in the pages of the mainstream literary canon. I recognised those characters and felt intimately connected to them, even if they did hail from the other side of the Atlantic (often via some manifestation of the Middle Passage).

Toni Morrison, whose book of collected essays, *Mouth Full of Blood*, was published last week, has always made it clear that she writes primarily for black people. It is the defining factor of her work, the centralising of African American life and its history, writing it from the inside outwards so that the margin becomes the mainstream. 'What was driving me to write was the silence,' she once said in a *New Yorker* interview. 'So many stories untold and unexamined. There was a wide vacuum in the literature.'[37] And she has filled that vacuum with a host of those stories, eleven novels to be exact, from Pecola Breedlove who tragically yearns for white beauty in *The Bluest Eye*, to the traumatised former slave Sethe, who murders her daughter to save her from the horrors of the trade in *Beloved*, and the blue-black belle of *God Help the Child* who suffers crippling self-loathing at the hands of colourism. Her predominantly female protagonists occupy spaces of consistent tragedy and ever-encircling oppression of one kind or another, but they are often courageous, or at the very least made visible and understood, which is a victory in itself.

Now eighty-eight, Morrison is America's most institutionally revered living writer: in addition to the Pulitzer and the

Nobel, she was awarded the Presidential Medal of Freedom by Barack Obama in 2012, the highest civilian honour available in the United States. But since the publication of her first novel in 1970 her work has had its fair share of criticism. *The Bluest Eye* was accused of fuelling negative perceptions of black men at a time when black men really didn't need it (which is basically never, and this implies concerning things about creative freedom for artists of colour). Other criticism has complained of her overzealousness with poetics and the lyrical, which John Updike grumbled about in his *New Yorker* review of her 2008 novel *A Mercy*. When Morrison won the Nobel Prize in Literature, the first African American woman to do so, the question was raised as to whether she actually deserved it, artistically, or whether it was more a case of positive discrimination. The mastery and luminosity of her prose have frequently been shadowed by her race even in its very devotion to it, the shadow cast not by her, but by the race-diseased world in which it is received, yet she has maintained a fierce individualism and commitment to the realisation of her artistic vision.

When I was faced with the fortunate and difficult decision between two publishers for my first novel, the presence of Toni Morrison on the author list at Chatto & Windus was one of the things that swung it. She was an example to me of literary excellence and sociopolitical dynamism, and also of what was possible, in fact required, on this side of the water. Black-British female writers, given the sheer size and scope of America and its much broader well of opportunity, have, generally speaking, been less celebrated on an international scale, but their work was a crucial element too in helping me to forge a voice. All writers, despite their various influences and comrades, are essentially and profoundly alone in finding their way, but the novels and poetry of Joan Riley, Buchi Emecheta, Grace Nichols, Jackie Kay, Bernardine Evaristo and Andrea Levy, among others, continue to carve a rich space in the UK in which the marginal can occupy the centre, in which that 'silence' Morrison spoke of has been filled and peopled with stories waiting to be told.

And British stories, of course, are different from American stories – the history is different, the scope, the culture, yet there has been a tendency in cultural discourse to examine black writing under a single umbrella. There is not one black experience, one black community, one black life or one black identity, not even in one country, let alone across oceans. By the same token, the idea that there is any such thing as 'black writing' is as absurd, reductive and impossible as the idea that there is such a thing as 'white writing'. There cannot be one without the other.

We are seeing a proliferation of new and established Black-British female authors coming to the fore, including Candice Carty-Williams with her debut novel *Queenie*, which charts the pained twenties of a Londoner negotiating relationships in the metropolis, Temi Oh with her sci-fi epic of six teenagers adventuring to a planet twenty-three years away, and Evaristo with her seventh novel, *Girl, Woman, Other*, about the lives of twelve interconnecting Black British women. Let's hope the trend continues to grow to the extent that it is no longer a recurring theme but a permanence. I will always be grateful for those sisters across the water who showed us their worlds. In among their footsteps, we are building legacies of our own.

On *American Fiction*

'I've never seen anything like this.' American author Percival Everett's delighted response to the movie adaptation of his novel *Erasure*,[38] under the title *American Fiction*, a sharp-edged dramedy about a novelist frustrated by the limits imposed on his work by racism. The novel was published in 2001, but the adaptation, scripted and directed by Cord Jefferson and nominated for four Oscars, feels thoroughly contemporary in its sardonic and satirical observation of a publishing industry easily seduced by stereotypical representations of black lives. What has taken Everett by surprise is perhaps the directness of the approach: the cinematic centring of a black male writer beleaguered by the tropes that hamper him, and the invitation to laugh out loud at the culprit of white ignorance.

Writer protagonists in novels are not always popular. Some see it as a cop-out – lazy, uninspired, off-putting, a failure of narrative voyage, even cheating. The writer should remain invisible and allow the reader to absorb the story in peace, without being accosted by the thoughts, feelings and experiences of its mechanism of production. But what if the writer *is* the story? What if their experiences, thoughts and feelings are precisely the material that the novel wants to display in order to encapsulate a truth about society? Or, if not to state a claim so great, perhaps the very position of the writer at the source of a fiction simply provides a useful conduit through which to observe nuances and extremes of human psychology. Rather than getting out of the way, the author shows the way, in person, in full view, closing a certain imagined distance from the reader, like the offering of a jacket.

The visible author is by no means a stranger to us. Anna Wulf in Doris Lessing's *The Golden Notebook*, who takes us through her colour-coded journals. Several of Stephen King's novels – *Misery*, *Bag of Bones*, *The Shining* – where dark corners of the authorial everyday make a convincing set-up for horror. In Chimamanda Ngozi Adichie's *Americanah* the writer is admittedly a blogger rather than a novelist, but a scribe nevertheless, offering her hot takes on race in America. Then there is Benjamin Trotter in Jonathan Coe's *Middle England* who is shortlisted for the Booker Prize, and the visible author of some of Alice Munro's short stories. More recently there is Rebecca F Kuang's funny publishing thriller *Yellowface*, written in the voice of an embittered novelist from Philadelphia who is driven to disastrous plagiarism by writerly jealousy.

'My name is Thelonious Ellison. And I am a writer of fiction. This admission pains me only at the thought of my story being found and read, as I have always been severely put off by any story which had as its main character a writer.' Ergo at the outset, in the first paragraph of *Erasure*, Everett addresses any possible discomfort arising from the visible author by aligning himself with it. Thelonious 'Monk' Ellison is a particular kind of writer – experimental, high-brow, therefore obscure, and somewhat embittered, largely due to his industry's inability to see beyond negative black stereotypes in perusing (and rejecting) his work. His books are little read and under-published, he would be broke if it were not for his day job as a professor of English literature, he riles at sightings of his books in the black sections of bookshops, and his most popular novel to date is about a black man radicalised by colour prejudice, thereby placing the theme of race in the foreground, when in fact, in Monk's own words, the hard, *gritty* truth of the matter is that I hardly ever think about race. Those times when I did think about it a lot I did so because of my guilt for not thinking about it. I don't believe in race. I believe there are people who will shoot me or hang me or cheat me and try to stop me because they do believe in race, because of my brown skin, curly hair, wide nose and slave ancestors. But that's just the way it is.

The friction between Monk's refusal of race and society's insistence on it is the basis for the film's radical jest. Jeffrey Wright plays the lead with skilful understatement, alongside Tracee Ellis Ross as Monk's sister Lisa and Issa Rae as Sintara Golden, the celebrated author of the infuriating new bestseller *We's Lives In Da Ghetto*. A stand-out scene sees Monk, having just emerged from his own poorly attended panel discussion, observing Sintara giving a trope-ridden reading from her novel to a captive audience at a book festival ('Yo Sharonda! Girl, you be pregnant *again*?!'). Meanwhile his widowed mother is developing Alzheimer's, putting pressure on his relationships with his siblings and raising questions about how to pay for her care. Answer: write a ghetto bestseller featuring an aggressive black man called Van Go Jenkins who can't spell, title it *My Pafology* and submit it under a pseudonym, Stagg R Leigh. It's meant as a despairing joke, a dig at the literary world, but Random House like it so much that they actually buy it for lots of money, then allow Stagg/Monk to change the title to *Fuck*. It's a hilarious premise for a story and makes for memorable entertainment.

Despite, and contrary to, the societal espousal of race that so annoys Monk, the psychological experience of racism has traditionally often been either denied or dismissed by those who have not experienced it themselves and have the luxury of obliviousness, with common accusations levied of 'having a chip on the shoulder' or 'playing the race card'. This can deepen the impact of the original affront and cause anger, which then may lead to further gaslighting. In *American Fiction*, the interior sensations of gaslighting and tropism take the lens, and are being milked for jokes that might have been less palatable not so long ago, when the subject of race was less casually discussed. We witness thoroughly middle-class, Foucault-ruminating Monk trying to do a 'black walk' on his (Stagg's) way to meeting a Hollywood producer who wants to adapt *Fuck*, and there are several derisive, well-observed exchanges highlighting his industry's hypocrisy and diversity failings. The film is part of a developing tendency towards the direct expression of marginalised creative pain as a basis for screen entertainment – other examples are Adjani Salmon's BAFTA-winning *Dreaming Whilst Black*, which charts a screenwriter's similar grappling with gatekeepers in the British TV industry, and Radha Blank's *The Forty-Year-Old Version* in which a frustrated playwright turns to rapping instead. It draws me to think of Toni Morrison's famous description of racism as a distraction, usurping energy that might be placed elsewhere, in this case, black artists making art about not being able to make the art they want to make because of racism, instead of making art about something else, and this is now supposed to be funny. It *is* funny, but there is no denying that it draws on the same well of black trauma that race has made available to us.

Things have changed in publishing since the watershed moment of 2020 sparked by the murder of George Floyd and the resulting escalation in Black Lives Matter protests, which led to demands for greater diversity across industries. There are more writers of colour being published, a host of initiatives intended to create a more widely representative workforce, and there is large-scale, general recognition of the importance of progress. But it is interesting to note, according to a US study, that while the number of black authors being published in the

US increased by 22 per cent between 2014 and 2020, 20 per cent of that was in 2020, with previous annual increases ranging between 0.01 per cent and 3 per cent. In the UK there was a 56 per cent rise in the sales of books by writers of colour in the financial year to 2021, but an Authors' Licensing and Collection Society census the following year revealed that just 6 per cent of living, published authors in the UK are not white.[39, 40] A feeling arises that the energy for change has subsided with the ebbing of immediate outrage, and although we are seeing an ever broader range of subject matter, a penchant does appear to remain in place for 'risk-free' books by writers of colour that perpetuate proven markets for their work, such as the slave narrative or the racial identity narrative or the gritty urban tale. There are twenty-two years between *Erasure* and *Yellowface*, but they share the same grievance against the publishing machine – although Kuang takes another angle.

The author protagonist of *Yellowface* is just as pissed off with racism as Monk, except she is a middle-class white woman named June Hayward, whose pen name shifts to Juniper Song when she decides to publish her dead Asian friend's novel as her own. Athena Liu died suddenly by choking on a pandan pancake, and so begrudging is June of Athena's bestselling literary-darling status featuring magazine spreads, TV appearances and large social-media followings that the novel manages to suspend our disbelief enough to pull off a most unlikely book heist: white girl from Philly pretends to have written excellent elegant epic about the Chinese Labour Corps recruited by the British in the First World War. It is of course a calamitous stunt, affording much gothic fluster (the author describes the novel in her acknowledgements as 'a horror story about loneliness in a fiercely competitive industry'), but it cleverly dissects contemporary debates about the value of the sensitivity reader, tokenism and the antagonism between reverse racism and positive discrimination. 'Do you know how much shit Athena got from this industry?' a narked ex-member of Juniper Song's publishing team asks her.

> 'They marked her as their token, exotic Asian girl. Every time she tried to branch out to new projects, they kept insisting that Asian was her *brand*, was what her audience expected. They never let her talk about anything other than being an immigrant, other than the fact that half her family died in Cambodia, that her dad killed himself on the twentieth anniversary of Tiananmen. Racial trauma sells, right? They treated her like a museum object. That was her marketing point. Being a Chinese tragedy . . .
>
> 'And if Athena is a success story, what does that mean for the rest of us? . . . Do you know what it's like to pitch a book and be told they already have an Asian writer? That they can't put out two minority stories in the same season? That Athena Liu already exists, so you're redundant? This industry is built on silencing us, stomping us into the ground, and hurling money at white people to produce racist stereotypes of us.'[41]

If I am over-quoting here, it's because this passage is so deliciously naked in its sentiment, so demonstrative of the novel's satirical exercise of self-reflection, so meta, and so basically recognisable. British fiction is not so different from American fiction on this issue, and I can recall similar instances of being assumed singular, representative and race-affixed. I was once dubbed, with the very best of intentions, 'the literary voice of multicultural Britain', as if there could ever be a useful or viable rendition of such a thing and it be a role I would want to step into. In the literary world my work has been referred to as 'post-race', or too nuanced when it comes to race, not race-y enough, though a crucial area of my interest as a novelist has been the study of how we wear our difficult history, how racial disease

manifests in modern life. There is often a military aspect automatically imposed on our creativity, an expectation of retaliation
against something monstrous and systemic, the effect of which
can be repressive, instructional, even thwarting. Did Peter Pan
know that he was white? Can you imagine his story being
accompanied by an exploration of the impact on his identity of
the colour of his skin? The fiction of race disturbs the natural
thematic innocence of storytelling, and risks there being no
room for nuance or experimental freedom or intellectual dreaming, such as Monk's imagined conversations between Derrida
and Wittgenstein or Joyce and Wilde, his symbolic contempla-
tions on carpentry and fishing, all of which add a surreal layer to
Erasure's fragmented, subversive narrative. I love these moments;
they seem to affirm the human right to the imagination, to reach
towards an existential liberty.

So perhaps there is progress to be made in self-reflection, in
encouraging the machine to laugh at itself in cheerful recognition ('what are we like!'). Via the kind of charged, exacting
comedy on show in *American Fiction*, maybe cultural industries
on both sides of the Atlantic will become capable of arriving at
an open road of steady transformation, where it is possible to
tell the truths that hold us back. Cord Jefferson, buoyed by the
Oscar nominations, has said he hopes the film will help lead to a
greater variety of black stories in Hollywood. Entertainment is
after all a forceful catalyst for action, not least in its own corridors of power.

Financial Times, 2024

World and Self

How to Tell the Children

My children have another mother. She looks like me but does not exist in a physical form. She lives inside picture frames and memories. She is a white stone cross in a cemetery a long drive away, which we visit periodically with flowers. While we are there my daughter makes some kind of arrangement of twigs at the foot of the grave, as an offering to her invisible aunt. Afterwards she and her younger brother play among the stones, chasing each other and finding sticks. It is a perpetual sadness to me that they will never know my twin, or experience the fun and opportunity of having her in their lives.

She died over twenty years ago, and were it an ordinary death – in as far as any death is ordinary – the matter of communicating the circumstances of it to my children would be more straightforward. Suicide is complicated. It's prickly, dangerous, loaded with potential pitfalls, mistakes and consequences. It poses a huge and, to the child mind, possibly indigestible question: is being alive a choice? Is here and now personally extinguishable? After years of struggling with depression instilled by trauma, my twin decided that it was. She made that final, irreversible choice and made her exit from this world and I have missed her ever since, every day. She was my best friend, my reference point.

In her absence my children are accustomed to an incomplete mother. The other mother, the completion, is verbal rather than visceral. She is a familiar history, a beautiful ghost who liked pink, who also liked to write, who had a quirky sense of humour and a kind, sensitive nature, and who is spoken about in warm and wistful tones. We talk more about the life of her than the death, but the death is so much part of the life – it is, in fact, for them, the story of the life, the main event, because it is what has deemed her invisible. Despite this, it has always felt right to me during conversations with my children about death that I would only reveal the finer details of their aunt's absence when they were ready.

On a summer's evening when my daughter was eight, we were walking to the shop to buy milk and a flash of my twin passed across her face. This happens sometimes, she looks a little like her, momentarily the likeness solidifies, emitting a particular glow, a little shock of resurrection. When I remarked on this to my daughter, she found the idea of it hilarious. 'Did you dress the same and look the same?' she asked. I told her that we looked alike but hadn't dressed the same, though we'd both liked wearing jeans, which she also found hilarious.

'How old was she when she died?' she asked.

'Twenty-six,' I said.

'What happened?' she said. 'Did you decide to play a game where you see who can hold their breath for the longest?'

Now I was laughing with her, it was one of those mind-bending, magical moments with a child when you are carried into the lightness and brightness of their existence where anything is possible. But this question also told me that my daughter was not yet ready. I told her that her aunt had died of an illness, which is a version of the truth. I tell my son the same thing when he also wants to know what happened; an illness of the spirit, which took hold of the body and became the director of it, like someone bad hijacking a ship. It is essential that I do not lie, that what I tell them always contains the truth in some shape that is comprehensible, laying the ground for the whole truth to come.

Through the years, books have been friends and saviours

along this journey, such as Isabel Allende's *Paula*, about the loss of her daughter, and Mark Doty's shimmering *Heaven's Coast*, about the loss of his partner Wally Roberts to AIDS. 'I used to imagine,' Doty writes, 'when I'd walk the dogs before Wally died, that the shining path the sun makes across the sea was the way the dead went, the way home.' It is feasible over a long period of time to gradually adjust to the most unwanted direction one's life can take, and for an altered person to emerge, clipped and a little bewildered, though with a steady, onward stride. It is even possible to exist with a sense of some strange and comforting inner energy placed there by the presence of another spirit, the merging of one soul with another at the desertion of a physical presence.

But there is an element of my twin's death that remains indigestible to me, even after twenty years: the actual moment of extinction, the breaking of the cord, the imagined pain involved. I try not to think about this, but when I do I enter a dark place that I immediately fight to get out of, a place without breath or calm as if someone has suddenly put a sheet over my head. Aside from this there is excruciating loneliness, which is both soothed and exacerbated by my children. In a sense, they are the ultimate reference point, a much more pressing one, their needs providing a signpost and their love pouring endlessly into the empty space. In another sense, though, that empty space harbours its emptiness in order to recognise its original nature. Loneliness is self-knowledge, a kind of completion, and in the context of family life its value as such can often be forgotten.

Recently my daughter turned thirteen. Her limbs have lengthened. She has acquired a fullness and a force of personality that seems deeply rooted in herself, capable of holding the information of the death, the reason behind her aunt's absence, without being accosted by it. I have had to be as sure as possible that the information will remain contained in someone else's life, that it will not leak into her life (the child as repetition, a second coming). By chance, I come across a radio interview with the mother of James Bulger, in which she talks about not shielding her surviving children from reports of their brother's murder on the TV news. The stoic honesty of this approach stays with me. Sometimes the outside world gives us signs, and this seems to me a cue to finally lift the shield.

That evening, I sit down with my daughter in a quiet room and tell her carefully of our tragedy. I do not give the precise logistics of the taking of the life – the method, the moment of extinction – because they do not seem essential, helpful or entirely relevant. What is important is that she knows about hope, and remembers to try to reach for it when it is most needed. As we are talking I imagine that my twin is in our midst, offering words and insights, helping me find the right language. My daughter listens with her wide, clear eyes and her enduring innocence.

'Sadness can be too much for a person,' I tell her, 'and they want to go away and leave the world behind.' For us, though, this is not an option. You talk to someone or you do something that you love to do. And then we talk for a while about the things we love to do, such as making planets out of paper and hanging them from the ceiling or walking among trees or dancing around to loud music. During this conversation, it seems that my daughter and I are becoming closer, that we are crossing a bridge together to an open space we both recognise. In her lightness of being, she understands, and she deeply loves the woman she lost yet never knew but somehow still knows.

'Those flowers in my room,' she says, 'the tall ones on my desk – which one do you think she'd like?'

'You choose,' I say.

The next time we go to the cemetery, she brings the tall yellow flower from her room and places it in the ground before the cross with new awareness. The sun shines harder for a moment through the big tree in the distance, which is where I always imagine that an essence of my twin resides, rather than in the ground. The movement of its leaves or a rustle of wind through its branches are like a smile in reply, an acknowledgement. This is how she speaks to us. She is bigger than life, beyond us and within us at the same time.

Red, 2018

Travelling with My Daughter

I have a good friend in America. She lives with her husband in a lone house set in acres of open land which they own, the trees, the hills, the distance even, and the shallow ponds and the dips and holes where beavers peep in and out. Sometimes she sends me pictures of these diminishing creatures, with a sense of affinity and wonder at being able to witness them in what is effectively her garden. It is a wonder to me also, this act of buying land and dreaming on it a house, which through a long process of design, architecture and construction becomes a reality. Unless you are extremely wealthy, this is not the kind of thing that happens in London or its surroundings. You cannot own the distance.

Before the house was built, when my daughter was seven, I took her with me to visit my friend. At that time she was living in an interim house next to the land, at the edge of the Catskill Mountain village of Margaretville in Delaware County, Upstate New York. It is a quaint, verdant, bohemian place full of turreted clapboard houses, verandas and old-fashioned storefronts, the Main Street running through it serving around six hundred inhabitants. My friend, originally from Washington DC, had moved there from Brixton after deciding to return home to the US, this time to a rural location, for health reasons. I was intrigued and inspired by her resolution to make a different life for herself in a new place. I wanted my daughter to see the grand story of her venture, the power and liberation of it, as possibly some important contribution to the building of her character. It would be my first time travelling alone with a child, which felt like an act of power, the two of us, voyaging together across the world.

My friend and I had met ten years before while students together on the MA in Creative Writing at the University of East Anglia. If opposites attract, this was a prime example: she is loud and gregarious, I am softly spoken and introverted; she is someone who seems to charge about the world taking care of business, I take cautious steps and am fond of the familiar, if simultaneously prone to wanderlust. In fact, it is the contradictions within us where we are alike; we recognise each other's fears and provide a balancing effect or a helpful, discursive mirror. After graduating, we had remained friends and supported each other's writing. We would send each other drafts of chapters from novels we were working on and give each other feedback. She became an important part of my writing process, playing the crucial role of helping to restore faith in a project when I was running low out of exhaustion or the at times brutal isolation of the writing life. Someone else's perspective on an imagined world in your head can be clarifying and steering.

The interim house, in which my friend and her husband lived before their own house was built on their fifty acres, was a beautiful light grey with a turret and a hammock and five bedrooms and a stream rushing by. The first thing we did when we got there, after unloading our luggage, was walk to the ice-cream parlour, it being July, and a little girl in company, with a warm evening sky waiting to descend. We would spend a week here in Margaretville, followed by a second week seeing the sights in New York City. Throughout this pastoral prelude to Manhattan, I was touched by my friend's efforts to delight and engage with the mind of a seven-year-old. Often they seemed on one wavelength, both of them excitable, enquiring and fun-loving, taking pleasure in the simplest of things, such as swinging on the hammock on the veranda or walking through the chosen land picking blackberries, with which they then proceeded to make jam. My friend's quiet-natured husband was another easy companion; he is one of those calm, benevolent, gently detached adults who don't try too hard with a child and as a result win their favour.

It is often people who choose not to have children who know best how to be with them, and also who are the best company for their parents. Motherhood can have the effect of either flattening or deepening friendships — a certain strain or pressure is injected and a lack of honesty might set in, because of how much we are being changed inside and how little we really understand it, and can therefore articulate it. My daughter was born three months before I published my first novel, so I became a mother and an author in the official sense of the word almost in the same moment. These events both had a profound impact on my identity, on how I felt as a person in the world. I was newly affixed to a public and a private guise, the latter thankfully grounding the former. As a baby she was bright-eyed and rambunctious, not so difficult as I expected, she would sleep, I would write as she slept, I'd wake up a 4.30 a.m. and write for two hours before the day began. This is how I wrote early drafts of my second novel, which my friend would read and bolster. Our discussions about literature and the projects we were working on helped keep me connected to my creativity amidst the new milky haze of motherly duty.

Seven years later, we explored the land. We saw the marshes and the beavers I had heard about during long conversations on the phone. We picked and ate vegetables from the garden of the interim house. We went to the village library to look at paintings in the arcade gallery. In imagining their eventual home, my friend and her husband had erected a large white tent amidst the acres, complete with windows, an iron bed, colourful cushions, copies of *The New Yorker* on a side table, and in fine weather

they would sleep in this tent, which was something that particularly fascinated my daughter, the idea of sleeping out in the
elements with the stars and cosmos so visible. One afternoon
there was an equally magical drive through winding woodland
to a lake set within a mountain range. The water had a smooth
grey sheen to it, was cool on the skin. My daughter found a
stick — she always liked to look for a stick in a place — and
splashed around, unleashed, full of cruel and delirious mischief,
insisting we swim to the deep part of the lake and back again
then jumping up on us when we got close to her. 'What are
those blue lines?' she asked my friend. 'Those are dragonflies,'
she said. 'And look, there's some newts, and baby salamanders.'

Towards the end of the week there was talk in the village of
a tornado coming, though the day was calm. The sky will go
green, they said. We'll have to shelter in the cellar. We'll buy
cakes and eat them in the dark. So we waited. The wind lifted,
the clouds were increasing. But the storm, in the end, did not
come, at least not in the perilous way we were expecting.
Instead, we sat out on the veranda and there was some rain, a
mist formed on the mountains, the sky flashed, papers lifted and
shifted in the wind, but there was no need to go down to shelter
in the cellar. We ate the cakes on the hammocks, which maybe
rocked a little with the sway in the air, the man and the child
playing cards while we two women talked. Our writing journeys had been different since we'd graduated. I had published
two novels, while my friend was turning to writing non-fiction,
having found that she felt more at home there, more able to
make the writing soar and her ideas take the right form. I was
inspired by her perseverance in moving from one project to
another regardless. What makes a writer is the need to write, the
determined voyaging to the capsule that fits the words.

I learned once and for all, during this trip, that my daughter
is a creature of nature. Born and bred in a city, she nevertheless

thrives in the outside elements, in the wide green, fully alive, finding her stick, claiming the land. She had always hated crowds and loud noises. In Manhattan, she cowered. The subway made her miserable, its dungeons and clattering and dark tunnels. Fifth Avenue was a bore. The lead-up to this huge disappointment was a long, glorious train ride on the Amtrak down the glistening Hudson River, a dream of a journey framed by sloping lime and copper hills – but at the end of it was a torturous concrete jungle, a hotel room four floors up with sirens blaring below, and waves of ugly pollution. She spent some of her time crouching under the bed, partly in an ongoing game of hide and seek that she clung to, partly as protest in the form of retreat.

We went to Harlem, though, to Marcus Garvey Park and the legendary Apollo Theater and the Abyssinian Baptist Church to listen to a preacher in a blue silk gown evoking cascades of amens, leaving golden hope luminous in the pews. It meant something, to walk these streets with my little girl, where my artistic and political heroes had once walked, where Martin Luther King had orated for peace, where Langston Hughes and Zora Neale Hurston lived and wrote, and James Brown and Billie Holiday had sung their legendary tunes. My daughter was still too young to understand the significance of being there, but I imagined this rich history being communicated to her through osmosis, a tradition of creativity and struggle to be admired and taken pride in from an affiliated distance. She skipped past the stoops of the brownstones with her cornrows. In Miss Maude's soul food diner on Malcolm X Boulevard, after the amens, we feasted on Southern fried chicken, collard greens, rice and peas, and homemade lemonade served in an oversized jar-glass, which she sipped seriously through a straw. It is an act of hope to raise a child in the world, and with it comes deep terror. You want her to arrive safely at herself, her inner nature intact, her feet on solid ground.

The finale of the trip was a red-cushioned horse-drawn carriage through Central Park, where I took a picture of my fellow traveller standing on a wall in her summer dress, a lollipop in progress, skyscrapers in the distance. Now she rides the trains by herself. She knows the streets, has a schedule, a French dictionary, a phone, a bus pass, yet remains what she has always been, hates crowds, always finds a stick. That unforgettable sojourn in America is now a part of her tapestry, her childhood history: the access it gave her to another way of life, to other adults who would become figures of both wisdom and lasting friendship. The bond between my friend and my daughter still exists despite all the years and space between them. The door of the house in the Catskills is open, if she should ever wander that way on her journey, exploring the world alone.

Red, 2020

Yoga Power

There's a scene in the hit TV drama *I May Destroy You* where Michaela Coel, in underwear, is captured in an acrobatic-looking yogic backbend on a wooden floor, apparently performing her morning practice, while checking her phone. In another television moment, Issa Rae's character in *Insecure* has a girlfriend round for a daytime yoga date in her living room, both of them side by side on their mats performing somewhat less ostentatious back stretches while chatting. It's satisfying to see these random demonstrations of the presence of yoga in the lives of black women, especially as it is an activity most commonly associated with bendy, skinny white women in leggings and crop tops, happily paying as much as twenty pounds for an hour of ultra-sweaty, calorie-shedding Bikram or muscle-carving vinyasa flow.

I have been practising yoga for around twenty years, starting with taking ashtanga classes in London with my older sister, who is a long-time yoga teacher and practitioner. We would meet at eight or nine in the morning on some street corner in Euston or London Bridge, mist rising from the freezing pavement, our mats tucked under our arms, and undergo an hour and a half of Mysore self-practice (the form of practice where the ashtanga postures are carried out at your own pace) in an incensed, steamy hall full of deep-throated *ujjayi* breathing, an instructor walking around performing adjustments. Once my sister had trained to become a teacher herself and joined the world of the instructors, I would sometimes go to her classes and relish the feeling of being guided by her gentle, wise and familiar voice. She would hoist her roped hair up on the crown of her head and, cross-legged, straight-backed, manoeuvre us towards the alignment of our bodies and spirits. Yoga, she maintains, is an invaluable form of mind training and emotional regulation, a lesson in self-acceptance and the art of transformation – it's about much more than just toning and strengthening. It's a way of life.

These days most of my yoga takes place in the living room, on a non-slip mat rolled out on top of a rug, a couple of mornings a week, accompanied by music (suitable soundscapes: Tracy Chapman, Morcheeba, Lucky Dube, Passenger, KT Tunstall, John Legend's first album *Get Lifted*, Athlete's second album *Tourist*). It's always better in the purity of morning than in the cluttered fatigue of the evening. I banish my phone while doing it and am usually alone, facing the windows. I go through the entirety of the ashtanga primary series – the first and easiest of six, the sixth being virtually superhuman – learned over many sessions of following David Swenson's instructional DVD, *Ashtanga Yoga: The Complete First Series*. There are those acrobatic-type, elastic-hipped contortionist *asanas* that I have accepted I will never be able to do, and that's fine. I breathe deeply throughout. I count the breaths. I follow the logical journey of the movements as they work through the whole body system, and afterwards I sit cross-legged and straight-backed, connecting within, taking in the morning light. I believe that the persistent regularity of this practice over two decades has deemed me calmer than I would otherwise have been; it has helped me withstand deaths and other losses, heartbreaks, anxiety, low self-esteem, the world state and deep stress. It's so much a part of my living in and facing the world that if I neglect to do it for longer than a week, I feel a sense of gnawing unease. It roots my feet fully on solid ground through a simultaneous magical elevation.

Broadly speaking, yoga originated more than five thousand years ago in northern India, as a mental and spiritual ritual designed to develop inner harmony, awareness, acceptance and higher consciousness. It is not a religious doctrine but is a school of philosophy in Hinduism and a significant component of Buddhist meditation. Taken up in the West in the form of Hatha yoga, an umbrella term for physical practice, a variety of styles have developed, such as vinyasa (an athletic form adapted from ashtanga), Iyengar (long-held postures prioritising alignment), Kundalini (in equal parts spiritual and physical), Bikram (hot yoga), Jivamukti (vinyasa in tone and infused with Hindu spiritualism) and yin (which is slow-paced with postures held for as long as five minutes). Most of these I have tried, and found that yin was too slow, Bikram too hot, Iyengar too long – ashtanga is the one I always return to, the more strenuous, flowing, almost dancerly style linking breath to movement and which was popularised famously by, among others, Madonna, her desired result a hardened, sinewed physique emptied of unsightly fat deposits and fighting off the softened curves of ageing.

From its non-material beginnings, yoga has gone on to become a multi-billion-pound industry consisting of classes and retreats, accessories and equipment, clothing, dietary advice, celebrity faddism and a multitude of discursive and instructive media. The 'yoga body' is now something akin to the 'bikini body' – but originally there were no such things as a yogic shape or an aesthetic objective. This is an idea unleashed by the commodification – and typically Caucasian-imaged – branding of the practice. Actually, the mind is the focus; the yoga enables the body to exist alongside the mind, and vice versa, the health aspect is the most important thing. 'Do not try this at home!' was my sister's visceral response to the Michaela Coel backbend, expressing her worry over all those people who might be tempted to try it unaided and risk injuring themselves. As well as teaching in the UK, she has also taught and led workshops internationally, including three months in Rwanda working with female survivors of genocide and rape. Such are the proven benefits of yoga to mental, as well as physical, health that it has gradually come to be recommended by GPs and the NHS as a relaxant and strengthening treatment for certain ailments and forms of rehabilitation.

After completing my first novel, as well as buying myself a new chair, I rewarded the finished product of four years of writing with an ashtanga yoga retreat in Thailand. I travelled alone to Koh Samui to a group of thatch-roofed cabins and chalets set off a paradisiacal beach, and spent the next week lying on the sand listening to the waves or reading, in between tri-daily sessions of yoga and pranayama (meditative breathing), and eating the stern, holistic delicacies of the yoga diet: vegetables, tofu, raw foods, fruit, light grains, seeded breads. It was a peaceful and restorative experience, though tinged with a strange loneliness, that of being at the end of a novel, where there is, for a time, an abyss that you don't yet know how to fill – you are not yet ready to start something new, but you need the gap to be inhabited by something. The yoga was like a large clearing of the mind, the loosening of flecks and remnants of the last book, and I returned home to London ready to start on another, ideas for which were beginning to emerge in the beautiful stretching, the waits and the breathing and the counts. That strange loneliness, though, was also the familiar loneliness and alienation of being in the minority in the yoga sphere. It was rare to walk into a class and find a woman such as my sister at the helm, hoisting up her dreadlocks, leading the opening chant. She was aware that her industry was as Eurocentric and male-dominated as many others and she used her powerful nature yet soft-voiced wisdom to make her mark, to carve her own space within it. I love this contrast about her, and there is something special about being led through a public activity with someone who knows you well.

My favourite ashtanga posture is the 'fish pose' (*matsyasana* in Sanskrit, the ancient language of yoga), which comes towards the end of the primary series immediately after the shoulder stand (*sarvangasana*). You are lying on your back with the torso fully arched backwards, bringing the crown of your head likewise to the floor, chin in the air, the hands spread out underneath you with the palms down. Your heart is skyward. You are momentarily a mermaid. Every tension and burden is falling away like water, and with your heart so high you are open to all the goodness and positive energy of the universe. It sounds flowerchild and boho-mystic, but is a genuine celestial feeling that is completely within our reach. It whispers that you are capable of anything, as long as you remain rooted, present, wide open and true. What better awareness with which to navigate the world. How better to glide into a day than on the early triumph of a headstand (*sirsasana*), which follows the mermaid, your toes in the air, the blood falling to the brain, thinking of nothing but the breath, the in and out of what keeps you alive, and sensing that this is all there is.

Sunday Times Style, 2020

On Retreat

I have travelled to a few places to write. I have taken to seas and skies for sentences, to catch them in a different air. In the US to the magical Hedgebrook forest on the West Coast, that cottage near the sea where animals stepped onto my porch at night and I first found a way to leave the notes behind. In Ireland, it was an upstairs room in a house near a cemetery at the edge of a small town, where I wrote at a dark-wood desk by a window looking out towards the graves. In Italy, a signal tower at the edge of an apple orchard with mountains nearby, and the mountains seemed to help me hear the words more clearly. Then to a city, a grand and rustic high-ceilinged apartment in the centre of Brussels, which was a contradiction to the usual pastoral retreat where the sounds and presence of nature were a large part of the appeal. Why retreat from a city to a city? What does Brussels offer that London does not, and how will it help you concentrate?

It's a question that always comes up, even when the retreat is rural. While packing for another American trip, this time to a three-hundred-acre country estate in upstate New York in 2016, I asked myself why I was travelling three thousand miles away to write when I had just moved into a new study in a loft at the top of my house, a sky-study, secluded and silent, an ideal place to work. All my notes were there, the books and folders, the specific and meaningful pictures on the walls (L.S. Lowry's *Industrial Landscape*; a woman wearing a headdress of red-and-black butterflies), and the framed list of ten mottos for writing productively that was positioned to the right of the desk for difficult moments ('write every day apart from Saturday', 'follow scenes/images through to completion or exhaustion', 'respect your work – don't judge'). The process of packing itself felt like a kind of fracturing – the choices that have to be made about what to take and what to leave, the consideration of every possible scenario of thought that will mean you need to take this piece of paper or that workbook from when you were reading this or that novel or watching this or that film. You are transporting your creative construction site – the cement, the tools and ladders – and in the final wrench of departure something is lost, in the hope of something else to be gained.

So there I was on the Amtrak from Penn Station to Hudson, NY. It was October (pre-Trump, post-Brexit referendum). The Hudson River was to my right, a beautiful liquid sheet stretching across to the other side, the trees rushing by along the bank, reeds sticking out through the surface and above it all a soft autumnal sky of late afternoon, turning towards dusk. I had in my suitcase my laborious construction site of novel-in-process which over the next two weeks I intended to complete once and for all. Sitting opposite me were two women of a certain age, possibly sisters, wearing knee-length dresses and flat shoes. They had dried, papery complexions and dyed blonde hair. When someone in the carriage sneezed, one of them said, 'God bless you,' and they carried on chatting and sharing pictures on their phones. They had the effect of attuning me to the work I had come for, the painting of ordinary life in the context of black Londoners: they were so unquestionably, complacently visible, these women, that it was a useful and galvanising reflection of what was not. Distance can be sharpening. Watching the familiar from afar, the gaps become clearer, where to colour in, where to fill. As we sped onwards to Poughkeepsie, the sun moved out over the Hudson freed from clouds. Someone was swimming in the gilded expanse; someone else was fishing, a black silhouette quietly looking out on the water.

At the retreat there was a sculpture park – the organisers also hosted artist residencies in architecture, music, dance and visual art, though during my stay it was writers and translators only. Every evening at seven o'clock we sat together around the long dining table in the main house and ate dinner, cooked by a gifted chef. At lunch and breakfast, we were free to help ourselves to the contents of the kitchen. There was a Finnish novelist, a French translator, a Catalan poet, a Berkley academic, a librarian from Cleveland writing stories about taboos. It was a strange and strenuous duty communing with so many people with such regularity – I usually limit socialising to twice a week, especially while writing, as too much conversation has a scattering effect within, leaving me struggling to hear my own thoughts. I worried that the channel to my writing would be broken or disrupted, so I would walk over to the main house at times with reluctance. There was always wine, though, that staple elixir ever abundant at any official gathering of writers, loosening cerebral tensions, releasing gossip. We discussed the unlikely election of Trump and the recent foreboding shock of the EU referendum result. We aired problems we were having in our work, had helpful title consultations and 'difficult chapter' sessions, and I was reminded that contact with other writers is crucial to the writing life, that residencies are not only a place to work, but a reassuring access to our community.

After dinner, I would walk back to the neighbouring house in the dark, to my room that was coincidentally loft-like, on two floors, a desk below and a bed up a small flight of stairs. I slept long, bottomless sleeps interrupted not by children, just by dawn light in the attic window. On retreat you can be single again if you are not, you can pretend to be childless. Some mornings I would run through the woods and among the sculptures dotted around the fields, some of them huge, such as the spinning house at the top of the hill, mounted on a single supporting pole, and another house with transparent walls, installed on the frozen lake and accessible via a path beginning at the bank. Inside this house on the water were suggestions of domestic life – a platform covered by a blanket to convey a bed, a table and chair – a kind of apparition of home and a symbol of my absence from it. Despite the homesickness that tugs at these absences, the distance gained offers something valuable and pressing, if only a solid luxury of time in which to write. I did get to the end of the novel-in-progress, out there in the countryside near the Hudson, and it was a good end, the right words, the kind of end I had been hoping for. I don't know whether quite the same words would have come if I had stayed in my other loft back home. They seemed conjured by the open space of the rural terrain, the ghostly house on the lake, the falling snow in this vastness of America and my insignificance within it. I had forgotten myself, making room for more.

In Brussels it was different. Again, I was near the end of a novel, this time in the large-scale editing stage where everything is not yet fully in place. Again there was the complex packing and the wrench of leaving, but the journey was much shorter, and ended in another metropolis, right in the centre of it, near the famous square of Grand-Place that was just visible from what for the next month would be my living room. The apartment was huge. It was billowing with space, a living room, a dining room, a study, a bedroom, a library, a hallway so long and wide it felt like another room in itself, and so I used it for yoga. Downstairs was the Passa Porta Bookshop that was part of the organisation that arranged the residencies, and across the terrace the offices, workshop space and further artist accommodation. All this for the furtherance and support of literature. How lucky I was to be given this gift of isolated time and space to work.

The timing was significant. By now it was 2022, Trump had been and gone and was threatening to come again, and Britain had been shambolically dragged out of the EU at the end of the agonising negotiations that had taken place in this very city. It was a disheartening experience walking around with my silly new blue-black passport in place of my old, more dignified burgundy one. I was sad to line up in the non-EU queue at immigration and be made to feel so conspicuously and imprisoningly British. Indeed, the things that had been happening on that little island aside from the disastrous pandemic handling were not much cause for patriotic sensations. There was the frequent breaking of laws by the makers of laws, the policing crisis, the swelling poverty, the government-led stirring of xenophobia and racism. From the inside Britain seemed like a country in full-blown moral plummet and it clearly also looked that way from the outside, judging from the questions people asked if you admitted you were British – 'What is *wrong* with your country?' they said, 'What is *happening* over there with you guys?', and gave pitying looks. There was no mistaking it: I was ashamed. Being British in Brussels was bittersweet.

In the billowing space, I set up my station at the study desk and tried to lounge in the stately lounge as if it were home. Here there was no chef, I did my own cooking, which I would eat alone at the big glass table in the dining room. There was some contact with other writers in the form of book readings and workshops, but the structure of the residency was loose and entirely self-directed. Instead of running through open fields, I used the gym across the road and worked solidly through the days with the shifting spring light glowing at the patio doors of the study. It was fitting that the novel I was working on was about the concepts of home and belonging and where each of these is to be found, because on every retreat I have been to I have arrived at the same conclusion: that the comfort element of home is embodied by people more than place, that people make location, rather than the other way round. The need for the artist to retreat is driven by a desire to centralise the importance of the work, as if other things were in its way, but the resulting revelation for me has been that the work needs those other things (the love, the errands, the family, the distractions), in order to be a viable way of life. There is nothing better than emerging from a really good writing day (a thousand or so good words) and then sitting down to hug your child, with the burden of the blank pages lifted and your full mental and emotional presence in that moment; the initial joy of creative achievement is the writer's most amenable state.

The city retreat was no different in stirring that revelation, and possibly it was more so, for cities are inherently lonely. At the same time, they eschew any necessity of belonging on account of their perpetual transience, the anonymous passing through from one place to another, the foreigner is also familiar. In the context of Brexit sadness, this is perhaps a useful air to inhale, because it is a reminder of the antidote to self-annihilating nationalism: difference, multiplicity and the fusing of cultures are avenues to richness and opportunity, to the enormous power of connection, rather than ruin. An island needs the neighbouring shores. We are Europeans, and our cities are where we meet.

From the window of the apartment I watched the street, the window in the lounge with its high slant of white curtain. The people whizzing by on their scooters. Iterations of families walking at the slow, averaged pace of generations. The café workers in their aprons moving furniture out onto the bright pavement in the mornings. The young men in funky hats with bouncing strides and the old couples holding on to one another. In the distance was the bell tower rising up from Grand-Place, lit up at night in golds and silvers, the crowds below traipsing the cobbled streets buying waffles, truffles and friterie, or riding hired bikes along the lanes and hills, or simply sitting some-where, by a magnificent garden or beneath a canopy framed in a spread of leaves, watching life. On Sundays the bells rang out from the holy white stone of the cathedral, calling for prayer. In lieu of woods and fields, I went out into this playground, to ride the bikes and see the sights, the galleries and museums, to walk across the urban plains to Matongé where the afro barbers and Congolese vibrations reminded me of Brixton before it got gen-trified to within an inch of its soul. It was all relevant to the work, the pictures it gave of urban beauty, mood and hyper-activity. It offered a reflection of what I was trying to capture, rather than a serene backdrop of cosmic indifference.

Back in London, in the attic, there was another finished novel; I was glad to be home. Like the writer in Alice Munro's short story 'The Office', I have tried, several times, to find an office in which to work, but nothing nearby is ever quite right. I think this search for an elsewhere comes from some profound fear of facing the page, a desire to escape from the unknown burden or pain of it. Actually, the attic is the best place, because I know now that no one can really help you. You are alone up there with just your wings of thought, which is retreat in itself. Tracy Chapman was right when she sang, 'All that you have is your soul.'

© Diana Evans, 2024

Monarchy and Modernity

The candle flames were trembling. The pulpit was on fire. The bride and groom were waiting. As were the Queen, Oprah, Idris Elba and Doria Ragland, now the world's most famous yoga teacher. Just before he got on to the subject of fire, Bishop Michael Curry, the first African American leader of the US Episcopal Church, promised the happy couple, 'and with this I'll sit down. We got to get y'all married.' But there's a lot to say about the French Jesuit Pierre Teilhard de Chardin and his relevance to modern technology and the concept of love and how this relates to Martin Luther King, so he went on for another three minutes.

Curry's sermon was one of three moments during the royal wedding when I felt moved. I had not expected to be moved. I had expected to remain full of cold indignation at the pomp and aristocratic indulgence of the day, at the preparatory shooing of the homeless off the streets of Windsor by police officers who should be tending to more important things like knife crime and violence against women, at the £32 million shamelessly spent amidst the rising presence of food banks and child poverty. The first of these moments was Doria Ragland arriving at the chapel, a black woman quietly alone, being assisted from her car by a representative of an institution that had partaken in her historical oppression and was now required to respect her. The other was the Kingdom Choir's beautiful rendition of 'Stand by Me', in part because it followed the sermon.

Reading from his iPad, gesticulating, swinging his robes, smiling, rocking back and forth on his feet, Curry was a complete contrast to the solemn and stationary ecclesiastical address that had preceded him during the ceremony. Where there was stillness, now there was movement. For fourteen minutes he preached in the full-throated, uninhibited, theatrical and emotive style of the traditional African American church. He preached of Moses and Jesus of Nazareth, the Hebrew scriptures and the 'old slaves in America's antebellum South' who recognised in their singing of spirituals, 'even in the midst of their captivity', that there is 'a balm in Gilead to make the wounded whole'. Quoting Martin Luther King to begin and end the speech, this was not something ever before witnessed within the lofty walls of the pinnacle of the Anglican establishment at a royal wedding. This was a speech that could have been lifted straight out of the pages of James Baldwin or ZZ Packer.

'Just always be who you really are. Don't pretend to be someone else.' Words of advice from Curry's father, which he drew upon in preparation for this speech. An ardent campaigner for social justice, particularly on immigration and same-sex marriage, Chicago-born Curry, himself a descendant of slaves, did not tone down his passionate message of the social and political power of love in order to align with the reserve of his pale and stately onlookers. He did not filter. He did it black, with music in his arms, and rhythm in his voice, and a looseness and openness in his face that supposed an almost familial acquaintance with his audience. In his world, words do not travel alone from the mouth, with just their letters and their grammar for company. Here the body comes too, giving life to the words, lifting them into the air to float and dance into comprehension and human feeling. For Zara Tindall, captured open-mouthed in her pricey shiny teal in the pews, it was something to behold.

The expressions on the faces of the congregation around the church were also something to behold, ranging from empathy to bemusement to confusion to downright scorn. Four and a

half minutes in, Camilla Parker Bowles's ludicrous hat was
trembling as she held down her head: was she laughing? Prince
Charles was also bowed, red around the ears, more so than usual:
was he? There was half a smirk at the Duchess of Cambridge's
mouth, and when Curry exclaimed, 'Oh *that's* the balm in
Gilead!', throwing up his hands in emphasis, Queen Elizabeth II
straightened in her chair, purse-lipped, with Prince Philip at her
side. Meanwhile Oprah was swaying. Ragland looked steadily
on, a little sadly, as if aware of something of which others were
not, yet also with an innate sweetness, while her daughter sat
holding hands with her prince, occasionally conferring in love-
soaked whispers.

It was a sermon that will go down in history as a moment
when the enduring seat of colonialism was brought before
the Lord and questioned in its own house. In the mention of
slavery was the inherent accusation of white silver-spoon complicity, the recognition that this union should not go forth
without the acknowledgement of such. 'Love is the way,' Curry
chanted, in a rolling, conversational repetition born of the
Deep South. 'When love is the way, we actually treat each other,
well' – he put his hand on his hip and his elbow on the
lectern – 'like we are actually a family.' A utopia for our time
indeed, delivered with a grand humility apparently wasted on
some of its listeners, who were not quite expecting such blackness from a black bride.

Time passed, the fairy tale was slowly punctured. Here was a
wayward red-haired prince who had fallen for a sweet-eyed
American beauty. Here were colourful dresses and fancy hats;
mugs, flags, fridge magnets and coasters for adorning our homes
with emblems of their love. The expectation was that Harry
and Meghan would live happily ever after and eat cucumber
sandwiches with Queen Elizabeth. They would have lucky

babies whose silver spoons might one day turn into crowns or, if not, tiaras, or diamonds, or a nice brooch. When they emerged from the church, now 'prince and his princess', shining in the afternoon light, she resplendent in snowy white and he in his medals, it was the same picture as other royal weddings, only this time the heroine was a career woman and an avowed feminist.

On the face of it, Meghan Markle slotted into British high society with apparent ease and poise. If it vexed her that Princess Michael of Kent wore a racist blackamoor brooch at a Buckingham Palace Christmas luncheon, we didn't know about it, and her own presence, in its juxtaposition, did the work of highlighting a grotesque everyday faux pas that would probably otherwise have gone unnoticed. Following the wedding, she wore the right clothes and sat in the right way with her legs crossed at the ankles instead of at the knees. While Caribbean immigrants were undergoing botched deportations and refusals of re-entry into Britain at the hands of the *Windrush* scandal, Markle was an embodiment of the acceptable aristocratic face of blackness, pale enough to move through majestic luncheons and palace rooms, while at the same time making the 2019 Powerlist of the one hundred most powerful black people in the UK. A recent YouGov survey[42] had also posited Prince Harry as the most popular member of the royal family aside from the queen, and his new wife probably had something to do with it.

Any speculation though that Markle's presence in the monarchy heralded a step forward in Britain's detachment from its colonial past was as ridiculous as the long-quashed idea of Barack Obama effecting a post-race age. She was simply a woman who fell in love, and what seemed most at threat, most pressing, was the well-being of her feminism. Was there really space in 'The Firm' for a once-precocious activist who at age eleven got Procter & Gamble to change the wording for a chauvinistic washing-up liquid advert, and went on to become a UN Women's Advocate for Political Participation and Leadership? Is it possible to be a good princess, a 'good immigrant' (as coined by Nikesh Shukla in the book of the same name) and a good feminist all at the same time? For the marriage to take place at all, we saw a partial erasure of a whole person. Two months before the wedding Markle was baptised at St James's Palace by the Archbishop of Canterbury using water from the River Jordan, leaving behind her Catholic background. Rachel Zane of *Suits* was long gone, the acting career relegated to a few lines of her biography on the royal website. Twitter, Facebook and Instagram accounts were deleted, and in their place came Her Royal Highness the Duchess of Sussex, now speedily pregnant with the seventh in line to the throne.

Despite the sturdy matriarchal icons of Queen Elizabeth II and Queen Victoria, women lower down the ranking who exercise their own singular power have not fared well in majesty; it is not part of the fairy tale. Fairy tales require passivity and neutrality, which is why Diana Spencer, once she fully embraced her power, became an affront to the monarchy, even an aberration. Once Kate married Prince William we saw her gradual shift from a figure capable in the eyes of the media of modernising the royal family to a woman largely defined by her womb and her wardrobe. For royal brides there is one easy way to be royal, and that is to be slender, smiling, unopinionated and obedient to the machine. Anything else and you're a Fergie or a Diana, which is much more interesting (and far less detrimental) for the young girls watching but ultimately lacking in longevity. Could Meghan fare any better, or would she simply become another quiet royal waif, swallowed whole into luxury and impartiality, her dresses more important than her voice? Could she remain a part of that national gilded machine without losing herself? The answer was no, at least not on this shore, and not in the merciless glare of the crooked British press. The 'California girl' was eventually hounded back home with her broken red prince, where Oprah was waiting for a chat.

And the rest is history. An apparent frost between the brothers. Alleged cattiness between their wives caused by diva behaviour from the girl 'straight outta Compton' who has never actually lived in Compton. The British press continuing their merciless mauling of Meghan. The rumoured father and son estrangement and publicly disgraced uncle. Then, amid so much drama and saga, the global event of the death of Queen Elizabeth, at which her first-born son shakily, one might think, steps up and takes the reins.

'King Charles III' does not roll off the tongue. Almost eight months after becoming the UK's reigning monarch, and on the eve of his coronation, it still felt difficult to utter this title in full acceptance and seriousness. But of course, it was very serious. It was bank-holiday, Westminster-Abbey, one-thousand-years-of-history, many-millions-of-taxpayers'-money serious, and even though we were being pointedly reminded that this was a less lavish coronation than Queen Elizabeth II's, it occurred amid dire economic circumstances of which ordinary people were bearing the brunt. They may have felt compelled to ask, 'Is it worth it?'

Admittedly, the queen was a tough act to follow. There she was, a constant powdery fixture, waving and smiling when appropriate, addressing the nation from one mansion or another when required, brightly adorned in colourful, near-fluorescent hues as if to prevent us from forgetting her existence. Her head was on the money in crowned profile. We were aware of her every time we used a cashpoint, this white-haired great-grandmother dutifully serving in luxury at the expense of the very note you have just extracted from said cashpoint, not to mention the financial legacies of empire and colonialism. The morality of the arrangement was always dubious, but the staid undeniability of tea and the queen as two major tenets of Britishness endured – sweet, mild, harmless, even while associated at their core with some of the most egregious crimes of history.

Then there is the fact that King Charles III was taking the reins of majesty in a very different state of affairs from that faced by his mother. Whereas Elizabeth II was coronated at twenty-five in a cloud of feminine innocence and patriotic post-war pain, Charles was crowned at seventy-four with a chequered past and ungainly family dramas – a marriage ending in tragedy, the scorning of Diana, adultery's sleazy shadow, a brother recently embroiled in a sex-abuse scandal, and a mutinous, bean-spilling son. In the climate of our age, where the personal is public, the royal family has to work harder than ever to appear unobjectionable, and the tone of their cheerleader media coverage has shifted to accommodate this: they are distant, untouchable yet familiar, presented to us on first-name terms as people we might aspire to or even resemble – a human family, containing relatable, ordinary dysfunction.

This doesn't quite wash, though, against the pomp and ritual of the monarchic tradition. The theatre of the accession council at St James's Palace the preceding September, its near-religious tincture, seemed juxtaposed in the modern context, as if we were watching a series of roles being played by actors who didn't fit, who were not supposed to be thus flawed or tainted or real. The coronation ceremony would almost certainly bear a similar paradoxical aura, of objectionableness existing alongside purported sanctity, while Charles's estimated wealth touched £1.8 billion at a time when doctors, nurses and teachers were struggling to pay household bills. There is something deeply entrenched in the British psyche (reticence? fear? complacency? apathy – as well as snobbery and feudalism) that allows this scenario to recur, and the occasional energetic dissenter is met with a heavy hand by law enforcement, as witnessed in the aggressive treatment of anti-monarchist hecklers among the crowds.

But now that the queen has gone, a link to the past is broken, making way for the emergence of a new skin, a new self, for something that might be termed 'the Great British Nervous Breakdown'. Psychologically speaking, breakdown is brought about by an internal resistance to necessary, organic or inevitable change. Despite Team Charles's gestures towards a more modern, pared-down monarchy that brings 'the marginal to the centre ground', as he stated in his accession council speech, these careful, passing pledges may not be enough to make his reign a success, or to affirm its desirability. Republics are rising, Barbados most recently, with others such as Jamaica likely to follow. In the tumbling of statues and the cooling receptions to international royal tours that have been seen of late, it is becoming increasingly incumbent on the figures of empire to relinquish their jewels and look out at the real, damaged world from which they have luxuriated. The only way the British monarchy can hope to occupy a more digestible space in this time of seismic change, social unease and nervous Commonwealth is to make wholesale admissions of grievous bodily harm to the former colonies and appropriate reparations. Whether or not it is capable of doing so is a question of psychology, of its ability to adopt the new skin.

Guardian, 2018 and 2023; *Time*, 2019

George Floyd: The Heart of the Matter

We saw it. We saw a white knee crush a black neck. We've been seeing it; centuries have seen it. We've seen black strangled – lashed – lynched – boiled – drowned – starved – shot – stabbed – raped – locked up – and we've carried on with our lives, as if it were nothing to do with us, as if we had no part in it, as if we were a different story. One of the reasons this was possible is that the stories we were told and the stories that were most often placed before us, and therefore the stories that we often instinctively chose, did not contain the true whole story, the one about the knee on the neck. It was there, though, hidden in the sentences, in the absences, in the white space, in the wider background. And sometimes it was a little clearer and we might see it enough to acknowledge it was there but not enough to understand it. Understanding it takes living in another way, turning ourselves inside out, turning the world upside down, letting the golden towers of these old empires crumble.

George Floyd was a man and not an idea. The supremacy of one thing rests on the dehumanisation of another and the indifference of everything else. The man who killed George Floyd with his knee over eight minutes and forty-six seconds did not wholly believe that this was the neck of an ordinary man like him, a man who might enjoy football or a banana and mayonnaise sandwich or a particular kind of beverage or who had a childhood stretching back into shadows. He did not see a man under his knee, only black, only the idea of black, attached to a man, and against which he believed himself superior, possessing a worthier right to life and liberty. He was raised like that. We must blame him entirely for allowing himself to be captured, twisted and drained of compassion by the idea of white supremacy, and we must blame his accomplices for agreeing with him enough not to save George's life, perhaps even wishing their own knee could have a ride on that breathing, calling sacrifice. But we must also look at ourselves, our failure to contest enough the foundations of our own freedom, and to acknowledge the fact that because of it others are still not free. We went on living comfortably inside the idea. We were part of the indifference.

Stories are about people. Ideas themselves do not make stories. There must be breath, feeling, the witnessing of dusks, the fullness of days, people riding buses, people making love, the yearnings of restless souls and the endless preoccupations of the mind. Stories show us back to ourselves and open windows on to other pictures, other lives. Our gatekeepers have been selfish. For a long time, they have habitually made a dangerous and myopic assumption that we would not be interested in seeing the other pictures, in seeing the inside of what was invisible. They have been looking out of the oldest window right at the top of the golden tower and registering what they already knew, not what they did not know or did not care to know. And we, too, have been lazy. Why did we imagine that in any of those pictures of the invisible we would not see ourselves and recognise our own human feelings? Why do we restrict our vision, and succumb to the same myopia, and allow ourselves to be complicit in the unequal dividing of access and illumination? And why did we so continually fail to unlearn our privilege by considering what it must be like to repeatedly consume stories in which one is not included, yet then make do with that reflection at least for the duration of reading, thereby facing the lengthy, discouraging insinuation that one does not matter, one's life does not matter, black lives do not matter? All of this is part of the violence.

To unlearn privilege and give away power, that is what must be done. Do not assume you are the centre. Do not subscribe to the idea of the other. Open all the windows and look outwards – the further up you are, the more there is to see. Share liberty, share space. Make diversity and equality the default in the highest echelon of an institution. Turn yourself inside out and upside down. Begin again. Do not ask one of the black people you know what you should do about racism because they are only experts in its recipience, not in its solution. They can only tell you how it feels, and they have been telling that for a long time and now they are very tired. They cannot tell you how to live right after the cumulative deaths of George Floyd, Breonna Taylor, Mark Duggan, Ahmaud Arbery, Stephen Lawrence, Joy Gardner, Tamir Rice and so many other sons, daughters, brothers, nieces and loved ones, but only hope that you live differently and share this load. It belongs to everyone.

Harper's Bazaar, 2020

Bad Nigerian Daughter

Right in the deep of lockdown, observing the two-metre rule, my mother gave me a blue plastic bag, the kind you get from a small-fry, climate-change-indifferent London newsagent. Inside it were a jar of gari, a recycled hair-food pot containing an Oxo cube, a spoonful of tomato puree and some powdered egusi; plus a brief, handwritten recipe in broken English concluding, spurringly, 'You will do it!'

She wanted me to make eba and stew for the children, a Nigerian dish that she often makes when we come to visit. She was concerned about the absence of eba in the children's lives during the pandemic – not only during the pandemic, it must be said; rather, that the pandemic may have been exacerbating an already lamentable absence of eba in my family's culinary experience due to my failure to cook it for them. Many, many times she had encouraged me to, and a few times I had tried, always with the same disappointment of consistency, a dearth of a specific African transporting taste, which seemed to come from her hands, her skin and heart, from the personal history of its maker, and was therefore untransferable. My stews tended to taste like they were made by an English person, one of non-Nigerian origin.

I took it home, the blue plastic bag, without hugging my mother first. The junctions were clear, the London thoroughfares empty. I cruised past Hyde Park noticing its new blank beauty, no one riding horses, no sprawling families or crews of friends on the pathways, only a few lone joggers, needful of their flex. It was a different kind of emptiness to the routine city dawns or a quietness after rain. Here it was pervasive, silence everywhere, the world was stilled in sickness. Every day at 5 p.m. Conservative politicians gave TV press briefings during which they tried to persuade us that they were doing a good job of beating Covid-19 and made jarring efforts not to answer questions ('Will parents who don't want to send their children to school after lockdown be fined?' 'The schools will only be opened when it is absolutely safe to do so.'). Britain was averaging over a thousand deaths a day. Refrigerated lorries were being used as emergency morgues.

I'll admit, when the announcement was made three months into the pandemic that the schools would be closed, I was filled with anguish. Quickly, so as to allay the maddening bagginess of a routine-less house endlessly occupied by its children, I drew up a primary-school timetable featuring the standard classroom subjects: maths, history, geography, PE. The garden became a badminton court and lunchtime playground. The children's father and I took turns as supply teachers in lessons we were ill-equipped for. All life seemed interior, even when not at home – out in the low-peopled fields, in the stark supermarkets with their mask mandates and bleak, adapted queuing systems. Within this dystopia, sometimes I would take my mother some groceries, to save her going to the supermarket herself and catching the virus. I worried for her, living alone and late in her years. She liked to set eyes on the children so I took them with me. We would chat for a while, she standing at her front door, us at the gate, masked and gloved, having left the bags of shopping by her feet.

It has always been important to my mother that she preserve her ways and customs through her descendants. It is her duty, having come from an ancient rural ancestry, rich in traditions of food, language, agriculture and domestic lore, to sustain those values in her offspring despite the large interruption of England in their genes and environment. In our house when I was growing up, there was a simmering dialogue between English and Nigerian cuisine, with English the louder (Fray Bentos pies, horrible slabs of liver on Tuesdays, Sunday roasts). My mother lived an almost separate life of quietly prepared okra, of eba and akara, which my siblings and I relished, though which were often consumed, as I recall, at the kitchen table, rather than in the main dining room. Similarly, her native language was spoken away from the centre, in corners, in occasional phone calls home. She lived in the margin, doubly margined as it manifested both within and outside the house, and she therefore remained, on a cultural level, wholly intact, almost untouched, like a distant planet awaiting imitation or approach somewhere down the line, preferably by one of her children.

I am lazy when it comes to cooking. I will not make a white sauce. I will not make pastry. I will buy ready-made soups and ready-baked children's birthday cakes from the supermarket, at best ready-made icing. Eba and stew is, basically then, a professional-level exercise, requiring overly exact yet instinctive judgements of grain-to-water ratio and arduous, hunched kneading with a pestle and mortar – it seemed beyond me. And that's not the only area in which I fail in my mother's quest for cultural conservation, her wish for good, wholesome, Nigerian-influenced breeding of her grandchildren. I do not take them to church outside of Christmas. I do not take them to weekly Sunday school or encourage them to read the Bible. Nor have I ever attempted to supply-teach them her Edo language of southern Nigeria. Once, it embarrasses me to say, I even searched for Edo forenames on the internet because I didn't like the name she had assigned to my son, in the family tradition of giving new arrivals a Nigerian middle name. In the end, disregarding my suggestions, she supplied an alternative name herself, a little miffed, bewildered by my quibble. After all, she is not a shop where you can exchange an item, or a fortune cookie. The name, incidentally, the one we finally settled on, means 'Children make you greater'.

In healthier times, pre-pandemic, when the world was open and the planes in flight, I had travelled to Nigeria on literary work, for a book tour and some occasional creative writing teaching. Each time I go back it is an affecting and paradoxical experience. There is first of all the deep sensational gladness, pure and uncomplicated, at the approach of the reddish land through the aeroplane windows, as if I belong to it and am at last returning after a long absence. On the other hand, I am simply arriving in another country, a place in many ways unknown to me, in the same way that a part of my mother remains unknown. From a stretch of childhood spent living in Lagos, I have lingering impressionistic memories of a bright hibiscus haze in a well-maintained back garden, of heavy afternoon rain, and of the great fumy heave of central Lagos with its crowded markets and traffic-wading hawkers. My mother is a different being in Nigeria. She becomes one among the people – she's louder, looser – while I become the outsider.

On one such trip, I stayed in campus accommodation at the University of Nigeria, Nsukka, in Enugu State in the east, for a week of teaching fiction writing to a group of twenty students from across the country. It was a sprawling 1960s campus with a big blue library, outside of which was a sign in capital letters saying, 'NO COLONIZATION OF SEATING'. The writing workshops took place in a magnolia-painted conference room with green-framed windows along one wall and a row of ventilators along the back, Nigerian flags at the doors. We sat in circles on white plastic chairs, the students giving each other feedback on their stories. They had been selected from a thousand applications. They wanted to be Achebes and Adichies, to receive fellowships in America or Europe and follow in the footsteps of the great titans of Nigerian literature. There was a glamorous magazine editor who wanted to live in Italy, a bank clerk who wore ties and too-big suits, a published poet with strong Christian values, and a quiet, neat, excessively organised woman who was hoping to be a teacher.

Having taken part in both the teaching and learning of creative writing in various settings, I remain unsure about the worth of studying and publicly critiquing the early, in-class efforts of your fellow writing students: there lurks a tendency towards forced suggestions for improvement, for over-subjectivity where it is inappropriate or uncalled for, and it can be either fatally discouraging or distractingly inflating to the ego, sometimes with the effect of interrupting a writer's natural journey. In this scenario, though, I was reminded of the sheer fun that the presence of other writers can be, knocking ideas around, tossing experiments of language and narrative between one another. Here there was both a passionate honesty and a genuine desire to express an opinion, regardless of how it might land. The bank clerk pointed out that someone's protagonist was not filled out enough as a believable character: 'We have to know more about him. What does he watch on TV, for instance? How much money does he have?' This developed into a discussion of the transparency of economics in characterisation, of class factors and the treatment of backstory. Then the glamorous magazine editor was chastised by the Christian poet for maternal immorality. 'The woman cannot be a good mother at the end,' he said. 'She cannot look after the children well, because she doesn't know how to pray.'

At this point, laughter burst from the group. The writer defended herself by saying it was not about morality or religion, but about this one particular person who does not have to be the same as you, and does not have to think the same way as you. There was a swelling of feminist feeling, which deepened when it came to the poet's turn to get feedback: people were unimpressed with his recurring imagery of singing breasts. 'Breasts cannot sing!' the magazine editor cried, others chiming in agreement. More laughter and, becoming flustered, the poet tried to explain, 'I am talking about the air! The voices in the air around the woman. You are misunderstanding it.'

'Well, when you are describing something you should be clearer about what you are trying to say,' the quiet woman who wanted to be a teacher said. In other moments during the workshop, there were allegorical comments like, 'This one is too dense for my teeth to crack' and, 'There is too much salt in the soup,' which added to the joking, though the group was still held together by a level of artistic seriousness. I didn't make it, during that trip, to visit my relatives to the north of Nsukka in Abuja, or in Benin City which is in nearby Edo State, or in my mother's home village. This seemed a major oversight, intensifying the internal distance between being and belonging here. So too did my limited knowledge of Nigerian geography, history and politics; I had brought along with me the fourth volume of Oshomha Imoagene's Know Your Country Series, *The Edo and their Neighbours of M. Western Nigeria*, which I had been reading before leaving the UK, but the fact of the matter remained that there was lots I didn't know about my other country. Although I had not been a resident of Nigeria since the age of ten, and at that only for three years, I felt a nagging obligation, as well as an expectation, to prove my connection to the place, the existence of some long, esoteric merging through a process of osmosis from mother to daughter. Inadequacy walked with me. A familiar alienation endured, the quintessential, dull remove of the second generation: black in Britain, British in Nigeria. The self becomes entangled in a popular dichotomy of identity, an overriding, useless need to posit someone as one thing or another thing, to make someone fit in.

I was once asked to write a feature for *Grazia* magazine about the experience of being mixed-race. At the time I was instinctively reluctant to accept the commission. It is usually people who are not racialised as white who are called on to openly contemplate or describe the condition of being whatever society has labelled you as, to take an awkward, external view of themselves, as if it is possible to watch yourself walking by from a window. This is what it felt like writing that *Grazia* article, which I later realised was a mistake. It was a struggle to write – unwieldly, over-strenuous, unnatural. It was like trying to articulate a veneer, like the colour blue explaining its perceived rather than known blueness. There is an inference at play in this kind of ethnic divulgence that you are something else, something other, and require explaining even to yourself. I sensed that it was not going to end well, and when I saw the headline of the published feature a few weeks later, for a short time I was heartbroken: 'Why Do You Think I'm Black?' it read. It felt like a betrayal, in which I was wrongly declared as the traitor. The correction printed in the following month's issue was futile. *Grazia* had epitomised a grotesque answer to their own question of what it is (sometimes) like to be mixed-race.

My book tour through Nigeria in 2005 was my first time travelling there as a published author and without the company of my family. While writing *26a*, part of which was set in Nigeria, I had intended to make a short visit back for research, which in the end hadn't been possible, so I'd employed instead my marinated memories of the place in their intriguing sepia hue, and found the hibiscus bushes at the edges of the garden, the red-headed lizards and the smell of leather and petrol fumes. The *26a* tour started in Lagos and went north (my first time in that part of the country) to Kano and Katsina. I was received warmly as a daughter of Nigeria once removed. At book readings I was asked faintly accusatory questions by members of the audience, such as why it had taken me so long to come back, why I wasn't married to a Nigerian, or what my thoughts were on the country's current political situation. It was my duty, I gathered, being thus removed, to stay attached from afar, engaged and interested as a virtual citizen, capable of slipping at any point into the fabric of everyday life in my mother's homeland. But as much as I relished being back there, I was also an example to people of what my mother had tried to avoid, the diminishing of one's country in the extracted generation below.

In the city of Katsina, my book reading was hosted in a polytechnic lecture hall with broken windows and faulty lighting and attended by the long-robed dignitaries of the area. Musicians, standing by the high table at the front of the room, played a traditional serenade. There were a series of ceremonial introductory speeches addressed to an overwhelmingly male audience, apart from a row of four women who were sitting about halfway up the slant of chairs, their heads covered in hijabs and their faces bright with make-up, wearing jeans with tight tops and jewellery. I felt embarrassingly unworthy of the level of ceremony being played out in the room on my account, but I was glad to see those women in front of me and kept my focus on them, a place of connection. It was late afternoon and the light was fading. The room got darker and darker as the evening crept in. In the end, devoid of electricity, we were sitting in almost total darkness and I could only see the women in outline, their bright faces gone to shadows. Who do we become in another place? Who would we have been, my sisters and I, if we had stayed in that house in Lagos with the hibiscus garden, and grown there into women? On a later trip to Nigeria in 2018, we went, two of us, to see that old house, now unoccupied. We walked along the street, stood outside and looked into the compound, remembering earlier versions of ourselves, when we could speak the Edo tongue. Were we less Nigerian now than we were before, or were we exactly the same?

Before the lockdown was lifted, I went for a walk with my mother in her northwest London neighbourhood, observing the two-metre rule. She wore her hat and overcoat, red gloves, a mask. We talked about how the relatives in Nigeria were doing. They were in lockdown too. We passed the front-yard pot plants and the hedges, the mint, the chrysanthemums. She stopped sometimes to articulate a thought, like the process of condensing egusi successfully into stew ('the more you do it, you practise, it is getting easier'), and the question of whether it is better to live in the countryside or in the city. She would not, she said, like to live in the countryside. She liked watching the people go by in the street. She liked a street, and a higher window to watch it from. She wanted life close, the comfort and community of it. This is her post office, for example, this red house with its signage. She gave a brief appraisal of the post office as we passed it, taking in the sight of the peaceful Sunday vans, ready for Monday.

She walked these familiar streets with a mild sashay and a faint skyward stance, a swing of the leg, a bounce, and I kept behind her at our safe distance. I have accepted that I will never meet her in the department of the eba. My stew base will remain too English, too oyinbo, my consistency incomplete. But it doesn't matter; there is more to inherit. An Irish fortune teller once read my stones, and she told me of a woman at the edge of her vision with fluttering white feathers. She was an old woman with milk-coloured hair and thin eyelids, this fortune teller, and she lived near a graveyard. She told me this, her eyelids flickering: 'If you go back and look into your mother's family history, you will be astonished.' There is more to discover, more to find. The story of the past is the story of who we are. Children make you greater.

Lockdown Dresses

The bars are closed. The libraries are closed. Topshop is closed. The swimming pools are closed. There are no laps up and down in the wet blue, no public showers, no public. Life now is private, formless. We are locked down in our houses, flats, castles, hovels and hotels while outside the world is emptier, creeping along its pavements like a sick yellow mist, a disease with long arms and high fever, coughing, emitting droplets. I am faced with ludicrous questions of the new danger: can I hug my mother if I ever see her again in the flesh? Is it safe for a teenager to go to the newsagent to buy Pritt Stick?

The Co-op at the end of the road smells of weed. Dark daytime souls waft along the aisles gazing into the empty fridges, at a single block of the least popular cheese, or a lone tray of sub-par chicken breasts. There are no eggs. There is no pasta or washing powder or tuna. There are lots of crisps, though, and parsnips. It's an interesting opportunity to survey the foodstuffs and groceries deemed either essential or dispensable in a time of emergency: we will survive on penne and passata and never, ever run out of toilet roll; if we do not perish from the yellow mist we may perish instead by overdosing on crunchy peanut butter and white carbs.

The schools are closed. The offices are closed. We are one with the daytime souls with loosened schedules and loose-waisted house clothes. No one wears make-up anymore – why bother? You are only going as far as Tesco, and in Tesco your face will take on that anguished, searching, haunted look that spoils make-up anyway; you will avoid other humans by two metres; you will be concentrating on evading droplets, and might also be wearing a face mask fashioned out of one half of a bikini top. One day at the supermarket I find eggs. It is like finding gold. I gather them in my hands, thinking of scrambling, frying, boiling, all the different ways of eggs, and when I get home my partner falls at my feet and hugs my ankles. It is decided that we will fry, to make them go further, we can each, the four of us, have a whole egg sandwich (albeit without ketchup, another thing which is hard to find, along with honey). We have a magnificent feast, savouring the yolks.

The school, the office and the leisure centre are in the house, all of it, everything, the computers, the lunch breaks, the dinner lady, the register, geography, maths, badminton and football practice, the sewing machine. In a lunge for an enduring kind of sanity that can withstand maybe months of lockdown, we stick almost exactly to the education timetable. Structure is paramount. There cannot be a little boy on the stairs languishing over a Nintendo Switch on a Tuesday morning while one is trying to make literature, or a slumped and doleful teenager staring into space. There must be bedtime and GCSE Shakespeare and PE, the only difference being that we adults are the teachers and the dinner ladies – suddenly I am aware of my deep mathematical deficiency, reminded of my life-long preference for the humanities and corresponding disinterest in science. Aside from that, though, I unexpectedly enjoy giving amateur lessons in art, literacy and Spanish. They are welcome breaks from making literature, which feels both all too important, necessary in this time of global anxiety, yet simultaneously useless.

The one thing I miss the most is solitude. Ironic, as solitude for those who are helplessly sick has become the accompaniment to death. It sits by the bedsides, barring love and goodbyes. An entire NHS volunteer army has been gathered to combat solitude, or more precisely, loneliness brought about by isolation. The solitude I am thinking of is a slightly different creature: lone-ness, a necessary sanctuary. It glints at the edges of these strange and freezing sun-struck days where the public and private have merged. Skyward there is solitude. The planes are down. The birds shout; they have all the blue to themselves. The trees are full of light and becoming those startling colours of spring – apricot, crystal mauve, hot pink. And the children on the lawns are also shouting, hurling themselves at the cold wind. Where a writer's solitude could once last whole days until school was out, now it is an hour or two in one room, or a long walk, or a collusion with midnight, or the making of a dress. A different way of working is emerging, another kind of loosening, where solitude is an intermittent luxury. The family shines out from the silence, their healthy hearts, their regular breathing and their steady warmth.

Every evening at six I would put on the news and watch the multiplying numbers of the dead. The white tents in Central Park. The new mass morgues of London and the people lying coughing in the corridors of overcrowded hospitals. The continuous daily tragedies of Italy, Spain, America, here. The great terror was watching the monster growing before us, around us, waiting for the peaks but the steeps still rising, further and further up. We didn't know what life would look like on the other side. The normality we returned to would be tenuous and slowed and, for many of us, poorer. There was much to learn from this, we who watched and waited on the sidelines, shielding the young: to cherish and respect our heroes not just on Thursdays; and from the fortuity of our safety, to accept less than what we thought we needed, solitude or otherwise.

In a tall section of my wardrobe now, there are seven handmade dresses – the lockdown dresses. I made them one after another during those long months of Covid confinement, the sewing machine out on the dining-room table, fabrics spread all around it, strands of thread and random off-cuts on the floor, and an audiobook playing over Bluetooth. This was how I found a way to be alone. While the activities of the perennially occupied house went on in the background, I would be submerged in the fabric and the literature, the one enriched the other, they made each other possible, the story needed the physical concentration of the sewing and the sewing needed the cerebral distraction of the story. Both were engaged in the making of an actuality that did not exist beforehand.

One of the 'dresses' is actually a jumpsuit, in a jade-green material that I found at a Peckham African fabric stall. The others are a range of colours and designs – there's a flame-and-mustard number with flashes of turquoise, a plain psychedelic green one with deep pinafore pockets, a subtle, sleeveless cream linen with a silver statement button at the ribcage, and a boxy boat-neck midi in a spiralling display of yellow and electric blue which sometimes receives comments in the Co-op. I have never been especially precious, outside of environmental concerns, about my clothes being repeatable, whether this dress or that shirt is also owned by other people; but there is something special about being able to say that you made whatever you are wearing yourself, about the fact that it is not readily acquirable on the high street, not manufactured, not even a product in the industrial sense. It is an expression of yourself, an act of the imagination adorned on your moving, breathing body. It's a primal way of dressing.

When I was a child, I wanted to be not a writer but a fashion designer. I used to draw pictures of specific outfits that came to me in dreams. I would feel an urgency to record these clothes on paper while they were in my head, in the same way that later, when I began to write, I needed to scribble down a phrase or a line before it had a chance to disappear. I still have these 'visitations of attire' in dreams, but now, perhaps because I have become used to building characters through writing novels, the outfits that come to me are worn by someone in particular. For example, there is a woman in a rust-coloured shawl and red gloves with a rushed way of moving and a severe expression on her face. And another, wearing an almost-transparent blouse the colour of champagne and a forest-dark, high-waisted skirt down to the floor, who slips through a doorway, out into sunlight. Who could they be, these people? What are they trying to communicate to me? These questions are the beginnings of stories.

The clothes I dream up are not available in any shop, not in their exact tone or aura, so I attempt to make them. This is a powerful reclaiming of a personal identifier and method of expression that has been taken out of our hands by the fashion industry, which, in guessing what we like, also imposes and defines what we like. But we can go further than assembling our looks from what is on offer from the rails or catwalks, to creating an original. Sales of sewing machines and garment-making patterns soared during the lockdown periods, giving rise to a modern 'sew-it-yourself' movement where more and more of us were returning to the needle and thread, to the lessons we may remember from our childhoods, our mothers, grandmothers, aunties and, usually on rarer occasions, fathers or uncles. It was my father who taught me how to darn socks – not a chore I still do, instead I buy more socks because life feels too short, but I have made a point of teaching my son to sew.

Another male sewist in my family was my Nigerian grandfather, who was a tailor. Sewing is in the blood: my mother taught her children how to sew, having been taught by her own parents to weave and use a sewing machine by the age of ten. I remember clearly from my childhood the black Singer sewing machine in the dining room at which she would manoeuvre her fabrics, bent over in steady concentration. It later became a tradition at family weddings that her daughters would each make a dress in the same fabric, which meant poring through the pattern catalogues at John Lewis, buying the right-length zips, the clasps, interfacing, lining and thread, and then, on the big day, exploding together in a spectacle of matching Ankara or African Dutch wax. Making clothes can not only make you more self-connected, the quiet and calm absorption of it clearing space to hear your own thoughts, but when done in tandem with others it can bring you closer to people, any tensions or creases are smoothed and ironed out by the persuasion of a shared creative objective.

While making those seven lockdown garments I went through many audiobooks: Imbolo Mbue's *Behold the Dreamers*, George Eliot's *Middlemarch* and *Silas Marner*, Thomas Hardy's *Tess of the d'Urbervilles*, Anne Tyler's *Saint Maybe*, Colson Whitehead's *The Underground Railroad* and Octavia Butler's *Kindred*—the list goes on. With each dress I wear there is a memory of the landscape and texture of the story I was engrossed in during its making, Hardy's rugged rural fields or Butler's tortured time travel. Clothes are an important part of storytelling, giving an insight into the social and historical background of the characters we are following, as well as into their inner worlds and outward personalities, what makes them memorable, what makes them captivating. At the same time, the clothes themselves contain their own origin stories, along with remnants of ourselves at the moments when they entered our lives.

After the seventh dress, I had become tired of sewing, and I put my machine and equipment away. I had travelled so many lengths of seam and hem and dart stitching that I could barely look at another dress pattern. Their instructional, step-by-step language was suddenly hard to read. As the pained stillness of the world receded and the everyday noises of societal activity returned, there was less space, less of the patience needed for that deep concentration. The dresses themselves, though, have become a meaningful aspect of my wardrobe. I reach for them when I want to wear something colourful or centring, or when I want to feel a visceral connection with my Nigerian identity, or simply when I want to experience the calm evoked by the memory of those quiet, intense hours spent locked in fabric and stories, when I was all dressed up with nowhere to go.

Aitken Alexander Isolation Series, 2020; *Elle*, 2023

Steve McQueen's *Grenfell*

In June 2017 the London skyline changed forever. One might not be able to see it from every angle, but if you're coming in along the A40 towards Ladbroke Grove, towards the Westway and Westfield Shopping Centre and the estates of White City, you'll see it: that huge, high green heart, suspended on its white hoarding above the lesser towers and rooftops, above the train tracks and pavements and the so many thin-limbed urban trees. If you can't see it, it's there implicitly, this change, in the general crooked nature of our horizon – the crookedness now has an unforgiving, figurative manifestation, evoking the deadly impact of unregulated, colonially entrenched modern capitalism. London can no longer hide the corruption that fuels it.

Artist and filmmaker Steve McQueen was mindful, on deciding to film the naked burnt shell of Grenfell Tower, that there would be an attempt by the authorities to hide and hush away the catastrophe. He was determined that, before the building was covered up, he would record the blackened ruins of this avoidable, forewarned fire that claimed seventy-two lives, so that they could not be forgotten, and the need for justice and accountability in their honour could not be forgotten. 'The question for me at the time was, how do I engage with this tragedy?' he writes in the notes accompanying the film's exhibition at London's Serpentine South Gallery. The answer was to visit the tower again, having first been there thirty years earlier visiting a friend (he was enthralled by its views). The answer was to witness, and beyond that, in the subtle yet substantial activism that art is capable of, to record.

An exhibit, an installation, a short film, an artwork, *Grenfell* consists of a single, roving revolving scene of twenty-four minutes, opening on to an aerial view of London, the beautiful jagged skyline, the tarmac-grey and cloud-swept blue of concrete and cosmos gathered around dwindling fields, neat residential blocks, industrial quarters and Wembley Stadium on a winter's afternoon. Filmed via helicopter six months after the blaze, it starts high and stays high, giving off a strange, fair-ride dizziness, yet slow, very slow throughout, so that the dizziness has a reflective, staring quality. There is a palpable, daylit horror as the camera glides onwards to its anticipated point amid the sounds of traffic below and city air. We are reminded of the everyday mundane activity the fire would have permeated, the innocent and oblivious living of lives in these neighbourhood streets, and how randomly they were taken away.

Except, it was not so random. There was an insidious economic design to the set of circumstances that led to the crime of Grenfell. Originally marked for demolition, the twenty-four-storey, 221-foot tower was instead given a low-cost refurbishment by the Kensington and Chelsea Tenant Management Organisation (TMO) that was completed a year before the fire with cheap combustible cladding that had been banned across Europe. Fire extinguishers were out of date, there were no sprinklers, escape routes were limited. Despite urgent requests from residents to address these shortcomings, no adequate action was taken, and the question unavoidably hovers of what action might have been taken if those residents had lived at the wealthier, top end of Ladbroke Grove rather than the shabbier bottom end, if the tower had not been home mainly to the poor, the immigrant or the black and brown, and if the overall welfare of these communities had been more valued at state level.

When the camera fixates on the charred carcass coming closer, the city noises are muted and there is silence. It is perhaps the silence of the TMO in response to those calls for effective action, or the permanent, irreversible silence of the fatalities themselves and the canyon of grief that surrounds them. There is so much in the silence, it is both deafening and haunting, the shock is in it, still fresh in that way that the indigestible never ceases to shock, and it is the quietude as well of respectful memoriam, which also cloaks the anteroom to the exhibition, giving it the feel of a funeral or wake. Up close now, the camera stares and slowly circles, showing us the metal window frames striped by flame, the bare structural skeletons of what would have been bedrooms, kitchens and hallways, the only physical suggestion of human inhabitation being the piles of rubble-filled bin bags on the floor and the real-time forensic workers in PPE going about their awful task.

In the same way that the building is devoid of life, the lens itself is devoid of direct emotion, only applying a clear, unflinching gaze onto an atrocity, demanding that we take notice. It reminded me of the scene in McQueen's Oscar-winning film *12 Years a Slave* when Solomon Northup is left hanging from a tree and there is a long agonising watching in which we hear the twisting of the rope and the groans of a body deemed worthless and unconducive to profit. The thinking that killed the victims of Grenfell is not a million miles away from that mentality. There is a crucial point at the core of our societal and financial system where not so much has changed, and McQueen repeatedly indicates that point, in silent fury, through the chilling power of seeing. Look what happened here, the camera says. Look at what was made possible. A simple invocation, and of monumental importance.

Gradually, the city noise returns and the camera retreats, the tower merges back into the crooked terrain, full of its broken hearts all gathered together in a single, iconic green shape. Outside the screening room the names of the seventy-two are listed on the wall. No corporate charges have yet been brought for these deaths; the conclusion of phase two of the Grenfell Inquiry is expected, at the earliest, late in 2023 at the time of writing. As Paul Gilroy states in his essay accompanying the exhibit, there are 'unsettling echoes' of the 1981 New Cross fire in the lack of diligence and care with which the pursuit of just-ice for Grenfell has been treated by industry and by the state. This is an added tragedy, sending the same message, and it will also be remembered.

Financial Times, 2023

Moral Violence

It seemed like a reasonable development. Karim Khan, chief prosecutor of the International Criminal Court (ICC), announced that he was seeking arrest warrants for Israeli Prime Minister Benjamin Netanyahu and Hamas leader Yahya Sinwar, along with two other Hamas leaders and Israel's defence minister Yoav Gallant, for possible war crimes and crimes against humanity. By this time, seven months on from 7 October, approximately 1,200 Israelis and 35,000 Palestinians had been killed. Both parties were accused of extermination, Hamas specifically of murder, rape, torture and hostage-taking, Israel of causing starvation as a method of war and denying humanitarian relief.

At last, a thread of legislative justice had needled its way into a situation that had gone beyond expectation, beyond alleged retribution. But then came the US response, marking a new low in its public support for civilian decimation in Gaza. 'We reject the ICC's application for arrest warrants against Israeli leaders,' President Biden said, standing before his stars and stripes. 'Whatever these warrants may imply, there's no equivalence between Israel and Hamas, and it's clear Israel wants to do all it can do to ensure civilian protection.' Watching this speech on TV brought me to think of the dangerous state of the political world-stage, of how in the pledging of national allegiances for the sake of national wealth and heft, our leaders, ever more blatantly, lack the ability to tell a simple truth. Biden's close involvement in Netanyahu's war (the US provides roughly 80 per cent of Israel's weaponry and has given over $300 billion in aid since 1948) deemed him incapable of naming the moral barbarism of genocide. Indeed, he went on to say, 'What's happening is not genocide. We reject that.' Perhaps he was worried that if he did not express such outrage, if he admitted the truth of what was happening in Gaza, he would be in the tricky position of accepting, in theory, the aptness of an arrest warrant for his own government.

And then it got worse. As a British person it's hard not to be consistently aware – remember Boris Johnson and Donald Trump's smutty tryst in the White House, all those very staged and very important handshakes stretching over decades – of the 'special relationship' between Britain and America. Characteristically in tow, Rishi Sunak also condemned the arrest warrants, calling the ICC's intentions 'deeply unhelpful', their timing ill-thought-out, an obstruction both to a possible pause in the fighting and to the complex project of aid provision in Gaza (which Israel was actively thwarting). He too raised the problem of moral equivalence between Hamas, a proscribed terrorist organisation, and Israel, a country founded on land grab, via the 1917 Balfour Declaration and the 1948 Israeli Declaration of Independence which left Palestinians stateless and led to the first Arab-Israeli war. 'There is no moral equivalence between a democratic state exercising its lawful right to self-defence and the terrorist group Hamas,' Sunak told reporters. Other, though not all, European leaders chimed in, citing equivalence as their main objection.

Marching along London's Park Lane the preceding February during one of the ongoing protests in support of Gaza, British complicity was a popular placard theme. The flags waved amidst the spindly winter trees. A cardboard cut-out of Sunak bearing its own guilty placard. *Stop the massacre. Ceasefire now. Free Palestine.* The unifying imperative was to bring an end to the civilian killing, a command echoed in protests around the world. In that crowd of youngsters, oldies, parents trailing their kids, stewards in Palestinian scarves, uncles in beanies, dreadlocked aunties, Muslims, Jews, students beating drums, people shaking tambourines, those whose families have been immediately affected by the violence and those who have not, and those mindful too of other, less publicised conflicts with huge civilian bloodshed and displacement, such as in Sudan and Congo – there was no apparent doubt about what was so desperately required: the call for peace, the need for justice. While the very idea of protest was being demonised by the Tory government in an attempt to suppress the human right to freedom of speech, it transpired that the open space of protest is where reason often resounds. Protest is the naked voice, expressing its power, unbridled by bureaucracy, and any attempt to quash it is driven by fear of such power.

Netanyahu and his supporters are keen to maintain that of the two opposing sides to this war, one of them is morally sound and the other is not. The slaughtering of children and whole families in kibbutzim, the murders and hostage-taking at the Nova music festival by Hamas on 7 October: morally unsound. But the killing of whole families and the bombing of Palestinian schools, hospitals, homes and other civilian environments by the Israel Defence Forces (IDF), amounting to tens of thousands of deaths: defensible, by default of possessing the moral upper hand. On hearing of Khan's intention to seek the Israeli arrest warrants, Netanyahu decried it as 'a travesty of justice', 'a disgrace', referring to the IDF as 'the most moral army in the world'. This was after – despite international disapproval and forewarning against – invading Gaza's southern border city of Rafah and displacing a further 900,000 civilians. This was amid reports of patients being kept shackled, blindfolded and wearing nappies in Israeli medical facilities, of broadcasting equipment being seized from journalists to prevent live coverage of Gaza, and the IDF raiding a West Bank refugee camp leaving more fatalities including a fifty-year-old doctor.

When is violence moral? A harder question to answer: when does violence become immoral? When the methods used are as brutal as those of the supposed morally inferior perpetrator? It is very difficult, perhaps paradoxical, to apply lawmaking to war, and the ICC have a labyrinthine yet crucial task in attempting to bring warmongers to justice. International humanitarian law – or the laws of armed conflict, as set out in the four Geneva Conventions of 1949 following the Second World War and ratified by 196 countries (one of the few international treaties to receive such unanimous support) – pledges to 'protect all civilians, including those in occupied territory'. Other standard rules of war state that hospitals, ambulances and medical staff must not be attacked (unless they are being used to harm the enemy, a loophole that Netanyahu has repeatedly exploited with frail evidence) and that religious buildings should be protected. The existence of these laws is the only institutional method by which civilian life can be shielded or rescued from without. If they are disregarded, it becomes a situation of 'total war', which seems indicative of what we have been seeing in Gaza. At the time of writing in July 2024, approximately 15,000 Palestinian children have been slaughtered, with thousands more trapped or detained, while the number of women killed stands at 10,000. In the two months since the warrants were proposed the overall death toll has increased to over 39,000, mostly civilians (these numbers are estimates; the actual numbers are believed to be much higher).

By rejecting the grounds for criminal treatment of Netanyahu and Gallant, America and Britain succeeded in digging themselves deeper into an isolating moral quandary of appearing to show support for genocide. Whether the arrest warrants are issued alongside those of Hamas leaders or not is beside the point, and to object to them on the grounds of equivalence is to imply that two wrongs cannot occur side by side, that what is posited as the demon automatically creates the saint. Netanyahu's apparent war strategy has come to present as defending his people by killing multitudes of the other people, and he expects to be able to do so with impunity. What was particularly striking in the pro-Israel response to the warrants was the level of hypocrisy and collective amnesia being shown by leading politicians, who apparently take no responsibility for the plight of Palestine and the part they have played in its traumatic history. The justifying narrative being employed by the war on Gaza is superficial — that 7 October was where it began — and fails to adequately take account of the complex history of the region, its decades of occupation and ongoing cycles of violence. In the face of such amnesia, truth and clarity are the moral ammunition. Genocide is genocide. Language is strategic.

The Sandwich

In 2023 I achieved almost nothing. I published a novel. I spent a month by an Italian lake trying to master the art of the short story. I wrote some journalism. I spoke at some literary events (which usually interrupts writing for a time anyway due to nervous anticipation and discombobulation). But in terms of new words on the blank page of creative work, I had little to show for myself. It was the year of moving my elderly mother to a retirement flat closer to where I lived, so that I would no longer have to worry about her falling down the stairs sixteen miles away, or being broken into in the middle of the night with only the stick that she kept under her pillow to defend herself with. So that I would no longer have to drive those sixteen miles and back to take her to a ten-minute dentist or optician appointment, and if she needed groceries I could get them to her easily while checking that she was all right; partly it was a selfish wish.

The process began in September of the previous year. Or it began long before that, when I first tried to persuade my mother to move. At first the answer was a consistent no. Later, she allowed herself to be persuaded, out of interest, to let me show her some flats, which seemed to confirm for her that the answer was definitely no. Time passed. Years passed. Her legs got more tired, her balance unstable. A personal alarm was added to her attire, worn around the wrist, connecting her to an emergency call centre should she actually fall down the stairs. Eventually she again allowed herself to be persuaded, out of interest, to look at some flats, by which time it was the September I've mentioned, a bright day with the sun on the roads. I had a shortlist of three places, all in large, pleasant, suburban blocks with communal lounges, lifts, manicured gardens and Telecare pull cords. In each of these three places, I had been able to envision my mother sitting in an armchair working with her wool, or moving about the kitchen. This was the barometer of suitability: whether I could *see* her there, being relatively content, knowing what I knew of her life and the person she had become on her long journey. I felt I had adequate enough insight to draw up a picture in my mind of what that place might look like.

I am not sure what my mother was thinking that morning when I picked her up – she was wearing her dark knee-length coat, comfortable shoes and a brown hat. I am not sure whether she had made some kind of decision, maybe that there is a time for transition and it was coming, or if she had heard noises in the middle of the night that had scared her, made her slip her hand under her pillow for the weapon. She was calm and smiling, matter-of-fact. We looked at the first flat, its one bedroom and pale-pink carpet, a compartmentalised shower signposting the previous (deceased) owner's mobility needs, to which my mother said, 'No bath?' The second received a similar nonchalance and dislike. It was the third response that surprised me, even though I knew this flat was the strongest contender – it had a certain unfussy loveliness, thick grey carpets, white glass-paned doors and a modern kitchen and bathroom. 'I want it,' she said.

'Huh?' I said.

'Yes, OK.'

'OK? Really?' I asked her roughly twelve times if she was sure. I was so overjoyed that we went back to my house a mere six minutes away and had sandwiches, before dropping into the little Lagos of Peckham to buy some of her supplies.

The sale took six months. We had a bad, cheap lawyer. We packed in irregular stages. Crystal sherry glasses and trifle bowls, old fur coats and bibles. There were layers and layers of living set to be unearthed, bathed in dust and darkness. A round wicker basket full of adult evening-class papers from the 1980s. Shoes in broken damp boxes and rusty gatherings of jewellery. In a kitchen cupboard, on moving day, my son found a bottle of vanilla essence with a best-before date of April 1999, a fossil, seventeen years older than him. By now it was the middle of May, and over the preceding months we had been preparing the flat for its new inhabitant – painting the walls, putting up cabinets and hooks, installing a shower chair, arguing with a series of builders over the widening of the weirdly shaped opening between the kitchen and living room. I was spending a worrying portion of my working hours on DIY missions and trader disputes, in the evenings scouring the internet for home accessories and finishing touches. The atmosphere of impending physical upheaval, even when it is not my own but one I am involved in, presents a major distraction to writing. For me, writing requires a settled foundation, a secure, liquidy disassociation from interruption or urgency. I did manage to produce some literary journalism while sitting on the floor of the empty flat waiting for a sliding door delivery; it is just about possible to write journalism that way. But as for *real* writing, those flashes of potential fiction waiting in my notebooks to be written, this was in a state of pause. The best I could manage were a few Lydia Davis-style shorts. Here is one:

> The only boy spent lots of time alone in his room, playing with the city he had made. In the lower darkness of the house his mother dreamed of living and his father had not yet repaired the fence he had broken, felt it was beyond him to repair the fence, could not do it. Instead he was gilded by sunsets and the concrete slabs below him heaved from the violent roots of the cedar tree, too large a thing to have been planted here.

I wish I could say that by the day of the move, my mother's old flat had been ordered into neat stacks of boxes ready to be transported. She had tried. She had packed two suitcases. But it is difficult when you have been in one place for a very long time and you have grown old in that place, lost children and loved ones and therefore parts of yourself. It is difficult to know where to begin and with what to leave. It was like moving a great ancient mountain, like turning the Earth with our bare hands. 'This is the biggest thing we've *ever done*,' I said to my younger sister, sitting exhausted in the kebab joint round the corner on a break from last-minute packing. 'Bigger than *childbirth*,' she said. On Sunday evening in the rain, with my car crammed with more of her things, I finally drove my mother across town to her new place. She had a sad and determined look on her face. When we arrived, she took a seat in her armchair by the unfamiliar window. There were boxes all around her. The walls were bare, waiting for her colours. What I felt for her then was a sense of warm pride and an overflowing compassion. She had taken a leap of faith. She had offered her trust and allowed herself to be unearthed.

That was the first thing that stopped me writing in 2023. The second thing was summer, the breaking up of schools and the unleashing of children from their merciful gates. August is the cruellest month. August is full of working parents waiting for September and Brits left behind waiting for good weather. The children are at home or out in the neighbourhood, and there is a gnawing lawlessness to the working week that argues with the concept of all-consuming cerebral retreat and concentration. I still believed at that time that I write best in an empty building, cut off from everything, any obligation to check on the current pastime of screen-prone human beings I have had a part in creating. I had managed the writing of three novels with this separation firmly in place, and summer was always the hardest bit, a quicksand in which I was held to the mire, unable to detach from the terrestrial realness of things.

That summer in particular, one of my children was about to start secondary school and the other was about to leave for university – both major transitions involving high levels of 'emotional labour' and domestic admin, the form-filling, the welcome emails, the uniform checklists and student tuition-fee invoices. Whereas previously I had maintained a strict rule of no family admin in the creative space, now I found myself reading an extracurricular sports booklet in place of morning poetry, for instance, or highlighting lists of stationery equipment or trawling through deadening parental emails, alongside taking my newly closer mother to closer dentist and doctor appointments. I was not alone in all this – I had a partner and siblings on hand – but out of a zodiacal need for thoroughness and efficiency, I had unintentionally taken on the role of project manager, so I was laden with distraction, and there is maybe a whole other essay here about gender differences in relation to thoroughness and how easily any discord arising therefrom is put down to maternal martyrdom. Ultimately, I could feel a crack beginning to form in the hard wall of distinction I had built between writer and mother.

The Portuguese artist Paula Rego made the statement, 'Work is the most important thing in life.'[43] I agree with her. Work defines who we are in the world. It gives us purpose and direction. It is how we manifest ourselves in the sphere of public functionality. Without it, we might come to feel like less effective citizens, taking up physical space with less power to define the shape of our exteriority. I think that what Rego was implying was not that family or the other elements of our lives are not important, but that those things cannot exist in balance without the fact of work. Every day she would go to her studio and immerse herself in her paintings and prints, the nucleus of her existence. When it was finished, she would come out fulfilled, capable of full relaxation and communication with others. I am describing here something akin to my own optimum experience of work and transposing it onto Paula Rego, because the satisfaction of and need for creative industriousness in the artist's life is presumably common across disciplines. There is no bliss quite like the end of a successful writing day, when I have achieved a good word count, when I have *travelled* through the words arriving on the page and lost myself in it. Achievement, according to psychologists, is an essential human need, next to food and shelter. Writing regularly and often is crucial to my mental health and, especially while writing a novel, I like to work as consistently as possible – days off make me nervous.

I realise that there are parents out there who savour August, who see it as a time of relief, a break from routine, a chance to spend quality time with the children, picnics and barbeques, days on the beach, water fights, extended camping trips featuring star-gazing. I understand the lift and lilt in the air and the summery suburban silence of children sleeping through the mornings or transplanted with their parents to the Mediterranean if they can afford it; but it has to be said that the school holidays go on for an inordinate amount of time, and by mid-August I am desperate for the routine to return. Families do not need to spend that much time together. They need their dispersings and distances in order to come back to one another ventilated of small irritations and tetchy dynamics. By September 2023, after weeks of dealing with the scramble of tasks involved in helping my mother settle in, helping the children towards their new chapters, and in the midst of these trying to write, I was on the verge of full-scale, agonising burn-out, gasping for retreat and seclusion. There was simply too much in my life, and the part that most belonged to me was shrinking. Here is another Lydia Davis-style short from that period:

> The new cobbler had no idea the difficulty of staying in business. When the sickness came they stopped bringing him their shoes and keys. A woman saved him for a time, made him shiny, he ate all the right food until she stopped loving him. After that he turned to dust. They can see him through the window, a shadow in an overall, bending to his work.

My friend told me about it – the sandwich. We were sitting at her kitchen table and I was relating to her all the above. 'Oh yeah, the mid-life sandwich,' she said in quick recognition. I hadn't realised there was a name for it, that stage between the ages of forty and fifty-nine when a person can become saddled with caring for aged parents and raising children at the same time. First coined in 1981 by social workers as the 'sandwich generation', in the UK around 3 per cent of people fall into this category, but the numbers are growing: 'Not only is sandwich care becoming a more common phenomenon,' says an Office for National Statistics report, 'but carers are finding themselves caught in the sandwich for longer'.[44] This is to do with an ageing population, the fact that children are staying at home longer due to rises in tuition fees and the cost of living, and that many people are choosing to have children later. It was comforting to learn that the situation I was struggling with was a certified, widely experienced predicament.

An important element of the mid-life sandwich, which affects its taste, texture and digestion, is of course the filling. For a woman, being flattened within the doughy weight of the two slices of bread is likely a substance in transition, undergoing the momentous internal shift posed by the menopause. Her body is changing. Her oestrogen is falling. There may be waves of heat,

spreading across her at intervals. There may be heat that comes
and then turns cold so that she is left soaked and shivering. Anxiety and brain fog, so that her thoughts become hazy and
unclear. Interrupted sleep, low mood, low libido, clumsiness,
sex pain. I have seen women in this transition looking out at the
world with meekness where they were once bold. I have sensed
their reduction, their growing habit of self-deprecation and
apology, while men of a similar certain age may well flourish in
the opposite direction, becoming distinguished and silver-foxy,
weather-beaten and 'experienced'. The reason why *Sex and the
City* was such a successful show is because of how flamboyantly
it rejects society's desire to relegate maturing women to unbeaut-
eous and sedate invisibility.

So at a time when a woman needs more than ever to take care
of herself, she is pulled in two directions of taking care of others.
Meanwhile the world around her flaunts its long-prized pictures of what she fails to embody. You are walking through the
mall on a Saturday afternoon and there is a giant undressed
woman in the window of Ann Summers, wearing a crotchless
teddy. You check your email and find on your homepage more
salutes to the latest most flesh-baring female celebrities. You
flick open a magazine and there are still the skeletal waifs pro-
moting eating disorders and the comparative absence of your
real, dimpled, lunch-consuming and healthy physique. Though
there is increased advertising now of clothes and sizes for ordinary bodies, the standard Western beauty ideal reigns on as an
overarching accusatory default. Women need a kinder, safer
society in which to age. Our bodies, our very eyes, are stolen
from us by the culture as a form of control, and by the time of
the mid-life turn, beauty has become a prison, targeted by Botox
salesmen, retinol, vitamin C serums, eye creams, liquid collagen,
chemical peels, hyaluronic-acid injections, hair dye, dermal fill-
ers, laser skin resurfacing, psychotherapy and much, much

more. Imagine if throughout our lives we had been told by the world at large that we are beautiful in our many forms. Imagine if the icons and idols paraded before us looked more pervasively true and representative. How boldly we might walk on to our later time. How we might strut and hold up our heads, full of everything we have seen and come to know, and how much more lovingly we might meet ourselves in the mirror, watching with fascination instead of terror the way our faces change and physically take on that knowledge, which is the beginning of wisdom. These faces, these bodies are the only ones we have, and there is only so much you can do to change it without breaking it. The most useful and practical tool a woman can have as she ages is self-worth.

The sandwich, then, is quite a mouthful – not a snack, more a large-portion, high-calorie main course. Beauty fascism aside, how should we respond to the multiple demands made on our time and energy while preserving our own well-being? Is this the time that we surrender ourselves, and give in to the new forms our lives are drawing us to fill, or should we attempt to hold to the shore that seems to be slipping away, leaving a place there to return to when we are free again and our labours are done? I realise increasingly that if you try to fight the organic, logical course of your journey through life rather than flow in its direction, you are at risk of becoming either crazy or lost or, at least, extremely tired.

I have always been a fast eater. When I was a child I used to shock my family with how quickly I could shovel through a meal without appearing to, and I am the same now. But this sandwich thing takes slower consumption. I am learning to pause and observe, to hold it in my hands and look at it, turning it around, noticing the texture, the taste, instead of charging through until it is all gone. Alice Walker wrote in *Now Is the Time to Open Your Heart*, 'You would not drive a car looking out the side window, would you? Yet that is what it has come to for many human beings; they are driving their lives forward while watching what is happening along the road or even in the rear-view mirror.' She is talking about paying attention. About living in the present moment, and that connection, that presence, is where our strength is, the fuel that takes us safely onwards.

After September 2023, I still agreed with Rego that work is the most important thing in life. I still agreed when it was Christmas five minutes later, and for one reason or another I had not achieved what I had wanted to achieve that year at my writing desk. My attitude towards the idea of achievement was shifting. Work *is* the most important thing, but there are times when the other components surrounding it take precedence, for just a little while, or for longer. Those other components are the great wheel of our existence turning, the image of who we are and how we live, and it is necessary at some juncture to stand back and look at them, to stop what we are doing, put down our tools, go out into the open air and witness the reality of humanity. An old woman, for example, in a new place far from home, and the slow, necessary assembling of what is familiar to her so that she can go on – her pictures on the walls, a clock by the kitchen, a drawer for her plethora of scarves. Or the closing summer of a daughter's childhood before she leaves into the world, the anticipation and innocence in her face, and the way her brother gazes at her in their playful, easy secrecy, where they can both be completely themselves. I'm glad I didn't miss these images, that I still have them to remember. Pausing to look at them, slowing my eating, has taught me to occupy a kinder, less punitive, less regimented, looser space, which is an achievement of another kind. It is not always possible to do one's work, and when it is not, it does not have to mean that you have failed.

Finally, there is lots to look forward to. The menopause, like the sandwich, gets bad publicity. Instead of the hideous disaster waiting for us at the end of our obedient beauty, full of rejection, ugliness and depression, I prefer to see it as a ticket to freedom, an opportunity for a woman to define herself on her terms. The transition we go through to get to the other side of who we are is made perilous less by the physiological symptoms it poses than by our society's failure to flow in its direction and to respect what it signifies. We are brought to think of ourselves as powerless when we are becoming more powerful, as weak when we are becoming stronger. At the heart of it is not any innate disappointment in ourselves, but the patriarchal system's lamentation that we are no longer what the male gaze would like us to be, which we are cynically invited to join in with. We should rejoice that we have come this far, and are free if we choose from the belittling glare of voyeurism. The gift of invisibility is that you find yourself in the dark, and you begin to dance like no one is watching. Your body is yours again, like it was in the beginning.

On Wednesday afternoons, in the middle of the working week, I leave my desk and drive to my mother's flat to take her to her seated exercise class. It's held in an old public hall off the high street, with pictures on the walls of what the area looked like in history. Slowly she puts on her coat and slowly she gets out of the car. There are about twenty regulars, also with slow walks. They use Zimmer frames, trolleys and walking sticks. They carry their strength deeper inside them to use at the end of their journeys. When the chairs are arranged in a circle, they take their seats and work out for forty-five minutes to big band and disco, led by a woman called Linda who has set up a programme of activities for the elderly in the area. It is rigorous exercise, lifting and flexing their legs, shoulders and arms, stretching out their necks and hands. Afterwards my mother emerges sort of windswept and happy. Any unease I might feel about being away from my desk on a weekday afternoon has evaporated. For this too is an important thing to do. I no longer have to worry about her falling down the stairs sixteen miles away. That is what had been achieved, the materialisation of a closer safety. 'Meanwhile death will arrive,' said Seneca, the ancient Roman philosopher, 'and you have no choice in making yourself available for that.'

Acknowledgements

Thank you to the following publications for permission to reprint edited writings in this collection: *Pride* magazine, the *Independent*, *New York Review of Books Daily*, *Time*, British *Vogue*, *Apollo*, *Guardian*, *Granta*, *WritersMosaic*, *Financial Times*, *Red*, *Sunday Times Style*, *Harper's Bazaar* and *Elle*.

I'm grateful to Poppy Hampson for initiating this book, and to the Chatto & Windus team at Penguin Random House for their continuing perceptiveness and hard work: Rose Tomaszewska, Clara Farmer, Asia Choudhry, Rhiannon Roy, Rosie Palmer, Victoria Murray-Browne, Priya Roy, Anna Redman Aylward. Gratitude also to my agent Clare Alexander who supports her authors so passionately and unswervingly, to Vimbai Shire for her careful and elegant copyediting, and to my valued writing community. Deepest thanks always to Derek A. Bardowell, M and M, for perspective and equilibrium.

End Notes

1 Elizabeth Hardwick, 'Its Only Defense: Intelligence and Sparkle', *New York Times*, 14 September 1986

2 https://www.tate.org.uk/whats-on/tate-britain/lynette-yiadom-boakye/exhibition-guide

3 Toni Morrison, 'James Baldwin Eulogy', from *Mouth Full of Blood*, Chatto & Windus, 2019

4 Martha Graham, 'I Am a Dancer', from *The Routledge Dance Studies Reader*, Routledge, 2010

5 For an extensive account of Black-British dance history, see Diana Evans, 'Dance', from Alison Donnell ed., *Companion to Contemporary Black British Culture*, Routledge, 2002

6 For a detailed account of the life of Vaslav Nijinsky see Richard Buckle's biography *Nijinsky*, Weidenfeld & Nicolson, 1971

7 Oscar Allen, 'A Bit About Me', collected writing shared with the author by Oscar Allen

8 Morrison, 'The Site of Memory', from *Mouth Full of Blood*, Chatto & Windus, 2019

9 Carmen Maria Machado, 'The Resident', from *Her Body & Other Parties*, Serpent's Tail, 2018

10 Letter to Peggy Kirkaldy, in Francis Wyndham and Diana Melly eds, *Letters: Jean Rhys*, André Deutsch, 1984

11 Letter to Kirkaldy, in Wyndham and Melly eds

12 Cited in Carole Angier, *Jean Rhys*, Penguin, 1985

13 Letter to Francis Wyndham, in Wyndham & Melly eds

14 Patricia Hampl, 'First Person Singular', from Ronald Spatz, *One Blood: The Narrative Impulse*, Alaska Quarterly Review, 2000

15 Hilary Mantel, '100 Ways to Write a Book', from interview in *Mslexia*, summer 2006

16 Mantel, *Mslexia*

17 Julian Barnes, 'Running Away', *Guardian*, 17 October 2009

18 John Updike, Foreword to *The Early Stories*, Penguin, 2005

19 Collected in Updike, *The Early Stories*

20 David Foster Wallace, 'John Updike, Champion Literary Phallocrat, Drops One; Is This Finally the End for the Magnificent Marcissists?', *Observer*, 13 October 1997

21 Cited in Adam Begley, *Updike*, HarperCollins, 2014

22 *American Visions*, October–November 1998

23 Dorothy West, *The Richer, the Poorer*, Doubleday, 1995

24 Cited in Emma Garman, 'Feminize Your Canon: Dorothy West', *Paris Review*, 11 July 2018

25 West, *The Richer, the Poorer*

26 West, *The Wedding*, Doubleday, 1995

27 James Wood, 'Out of the Ashes', *Guardian*, 25 September 2004

28 Excerpt from *Revolutionary Road* by Richard Yates, published by Vintage, 1961. Copyright © Richard Yates 1961, 1989. Reprinted by permission of The Random House Group Limited, and used by permission of The Wylie Agency (UK) Limited

29 Rachel Cusk, 'Making House: Notes on Domesticity', *New York Times*, 31 August 2016

30 Excerpt from *Revolutionary Road* by Richard Yates, published by Vintage, 1961. Copyright © Richard Yates 1961, 1989. Reprinted by permission of The Random House Group Limited, and used by permission of The Wylie Agency (UK) Limited

31 Hilton Als ed., *God Made My Face: A Collective Portrait of James Baldwin*, Dancing Foxes Press/Brooklyn Museum, 2024

32 James Baldwin, 'Preface to the 1984 Edition', *Notes of a Native Son*, Beacon Press, 1955

33 Audre Lorde, *Sister Outsider*, The Crossing Press Feminist Series, 1984

34 Mary Oliver, from 'Spring Azures', from *New and Selected Poems*, Beacon Press, 1992, reprinted by the permission of The Charlotte Sheedy Literary Agency as agent for the author © 1992 by Mary Oliver with permission of Bill Reichblum

35 Mantel, *Mslexia*

36 Morrison, 'Rememory', from *Mouth Full of Blood*, Chatto & Windus, 2019

37 Interview by Hilton Als, 'Toni Morrison and the Ghosts in the House', *The New Yorker*, 19 October 2003

38 https://www.youtube.com/watch?v=KKhk4gb-3RU

39 https://wordsrated.com/black-authors-statistics/#:~:text=

40 https://www.wob.com/en-gb/press/black-history-month

41 Excerpt from *Yellowface* by RF Kuang, published by William Morrow/HarperCollins, 2023, reprinted by permission of HarperCollins Publishers Ltd © 2023, Rebecca F. Kuang

42 https://www.townandcountrymag.com/society/tradition/a28747118/queen-elizabeth-prince-harry-most-popular-royals-poll-2019/

43 *Paula Rego: Secrets & Stories*, 2017

44 https://www.sunlife.co.uk/articles-guides/your-money/your-guide-to-the-sandwich-generation/

About the Author

Diana Evans is the author of the novels *26a*, *The Wonder*, *Ordinary People* and *A House for Alice*. She was the inaugural winner of the Orange Award for New Writers for *26a*, which was shortlisted for the Whitbread First Novel, the Guardian First Book, the Commonwealth Best First Book and the IMPAC Dublin Literary Award. *Ordinary People* won the 2019 South Bank Sky Arts Award for Literature and was shortlisted for the Women's Prize for Fiction, the Rathbones Folio Prize, the Andrew Carnegie Medals for Excellence in Fiction and the Orwell Prize for Political Fiction, for which *A House for Alice* was also a finalist. A former dancer, she is a Fellow of the Royal Society of Literature, her journalism and non-fiction appearing in *Time* magazine, the *Guardian*, *Vogue* and the *Financial Times* among others. She lives in London.